"Because They Needed Me"

RITA MILJO AND THE ORPHANED BABOONS OF SOUTH AFRICA

"Because They Needed Me"

RITA MILJO AND THE ORPHANED BABOONS OF SOUTH AFRICA

MICHAEL BLUMENTHAL
and
RITA MILJO

an aequitas book from
Pleasure Boat Studio: A Literary Press

Copyright © 2016 by Michael Blumenthal

Casebound ISBN 978-0-912887-38-8

Library of Congress Control Number: 2015937376

Cover photos by CARE photographers
Cover design by Lauren Grosskopf
Interior design by Susan Ramundo

Portions of "The Heaven of Baboons" were previously published in *Natural History* and *The Washington Post Magazine*, whose editors the author gratefully acknowledges. Much of the manuscript in its entirety was previously published in a German translation under the title *Zum Affen Werden* (2012) by Verlag André Thiele of Mainz, Germany.

Aequitas Books is a non-fiction imprint of Pleasure Boat Studio: A Literary Press.

Pleasure Boat Studio books are available through your favorite bookstore and through the following:
SPD (Small Press Distribution) Tel. 800-869-7553, Fax 510-524-0852
Partners/West Tel. 425-227-8486, Fax 425-204-2448
Baker & Taylor Tel. 800-775-1100, Fax 800-775-7480
Ingram Tel. 615-793-5000, Fax 615-287-5429
Amazon.com and **bn.com**

and through
PLEASURE BOAT STUDIO: A LITERARY PRESS
www.pleasureboatstudio.com
201 West 89th Street
New York, NY 10024

Contact **Jack Estes, Publisher**
Email: pleasboat@nyc.rr.com

in memory of Rita Miljo
1929–2012

so fiery a spirit only fire itself
could ultimately defeat it

Author's Note

"A lot of people have asked me whether they could write 'my book,'"
Rita Miljo wrote to me in late 2007, "and I said no, because I was
envisaging a story both sad and happy, but certainly mixed with a
lot of humor. If you asked me, Michael, I would not say no to you."

And so this book began. During the winter of 2008, when she first decided that I could write her life story, Rita Miljo began sending me her unedited journals and reflections, compiled in Phalaborwa over the past dozen or so years. These entries were only loosely organized, sometimes in imperfect and ungrammatical English, and I thus spent much of the next two years arranging those journals. I felt that—she being the brutally honest and unique individual that she was—Rita's and her baboons' story should, as best as possible, be told in *her* voice,

What you have before you is thus a kind of composite and collaborative autobiography—the reflections of a singularly brave and determined woman, along with the reflections of a friend and writer who, unfortunately, got to know her only briefly, but with great curiosity and admiration.

My job, largely, has been to try and do justice both to Rita's unique life and to her unique voice. Unfortunately, Rita died in a fire just weeks before this book was first published in both Rita's and my mother tongue, German. But English, both of our adopted second language, was the tongue it was written in, and I know that Rita would be both happy and grateful, as I am, to see it in its original form.

Michael Blumenthal
Morgantown, WV
June, 2014

Acknowledgments

I want to thank my wife Isabelle Leconte for her expert proofreading, which saved me from certain embarrassments no native speaker of English should have to be subjected to. Her attention to detail and her awareness of the nuances of English convinced me once again—in the noble tradition of Joseph Brodsky, Vladimir Nabokov, and Joseph Conrad—that you needn't be a native speaker of English to be at home with its nuances and particularities. I only wish I could say the same for my French.

I also, needless to say, want to thank C.A.R.E., and (though I never actually got to meet him) Rita's successor, Stephen Munro, for providing me, not only with the opportunity to develop a friendship with Rita, but with one of the most unusual and rewarding experiences of my life. The Center's efforts to save and rehabilitate the often-disdained and vilified primates they devote themselves to in many ways mirror the efforts of certain heroic human beings to help the ignored, the downtrodden and the vilified in our own midst.

Portions of this book were previously published in *Natural History* and *The Washington Post Magazine*, whose editors the author gratefully acknowledges. Much of the manuscript was previously published in a German translation under the title *Zum Affen Werden* (2012) by Verlag André Thiele of Mainz, Germany.

Contents

Introduction

I have been publishing books—poetry, fiction, memoirs, essays, translations—for more than thirty-five years, but I never thought I would write a book like this . . . or encounter, and become close friends with, a woman like Rita Miljo.

But this, I like to think, is no ordinary book, nor was Rita Miljo an ordinary woman. Nor was our friendship—that of a rather urban New York-born son of Holocaust survivors and a wildlife-obsessed former childhood member of the Hitler Youth—an ordinary friendship.

In 1980, a fifty-year-old Lithuanian-born woman by the name of Rita Neumann—later to become Rita Miljo—spirited a battered young baboon by the name of Bobby from a national park in Angola. Therewith began a thirty-year odyssey that would bring her into conflict not only with many of her neighboring South Africans, who considered baboons to be "vermin," but also with the South African authorities themselves, an odyssey she often recorded in meticulous detail.

Much like the work of Jane Goodall with chimpanzees in Tanzania, Dian Fossey with gorillas in Rwanda, and Biruté Galdikas with the orangutans of Borneo, but without a background as a scientific researcher, Rita began her rehabilitation center with the goal of nursing orphaned and injured baboons back to health, and, at the same time, she pioneered methods of reintroducing troops of convalesced baboons back into their natural habitat.

I myself met Rita, courtesy of TV's *Animal Planet*, in May of 2007, when I—who, in another life (and had I known, as a young man, that such careers were possible) would have loved to become a primate zoologist—went to South Africa to volunteer at her Center.

Combining Rita Miljo's edited journals with my own, *Because They Needed Me* is a chronicle of primate conservation and the intrepid and courageous woman who devoted her life to it.

My only regret is that Rita didn't live to see this book in print, either in German or in English. But Rita's true language was the language of those much-maligned and misunderstood baboons she so loved. And I can only hope that I may have done a little bit to make that language understood to our own not-so-different primate troop.

I never had a friend like her before; I'll never have another like her again.

—M.B., 2015

Part One

"THE HEAVEN OF BABOONS"

And those that are hunted
Know this as their life,
Their reward: to walk

Under such trees in full knowledge
Of what is in glory above them,
And to feel no fear,
But acceptance, compliance.
Fulfilling themselves without pain

At the cycle's center,
They tremble, they walk
Under the tree,
They fall, they are torn,
They rise, they walk again.

—James Dickey, "The Heaven of Animals"

I'm not supposed to be here—that is, people from backgrounds like mine aren't supposed to be. No, I'm not supposed to be here, with Dennis huddled up against my chest and Maggie grooming the hairs on my arms, with Sabrina on my left shoulder and Tortilla atop my head, grooming the rest of me. I'm not supposed to be here, along the banks of the Oliphants River in Limpopo Province, South Africa, meters away from wild crocodiles and elephants and hippos and the occasional lion, letting Sunamo do her backward somersaults between my legs as she chases Cory and de Jager around the cage.

No, I'm not supposed to be here—certain friends and colleagues have told me, perhaps enviously—with these orphaned chacma baboons, smacking my lips as I attempt to mimic their grunts and chatterings, trying for myself to understand how I got here and why it feels so good—this grooming and chattering, these small orphaned baboon bodies against my chest.

● ● ●

It's a long way from what were once the streets of New York's German-Jewish ghetto of Washington Heights to the bush of northern Limpopo Province in South Africa. It's also a long way from being the second-generation son of German-Jewish immigrants who escaped Hitler's ovens by the skin of their teeth to being friends with a woman who was once a member of the Hitler Youth. And it is, I suspect, an even greater distance from being an urban boy terrified of cockroaches and mice to being a middle-aged man with a baboon named Dennis huddled up against his chest, Dennis's sister Maggie grooming his chest hairs, and two more, named Sabrina and Tortilla, on his left shoulder and atop his head, grooming the rest of him.

But all this, in May of 2007, is where I am, and the amazing story of Rita Miljo and her baboons is the reason I got here.

● ● ●

The way I got here, as is the case with so many of the volunteers, is by watching *Animal Planet*. By watching, to be precise, their two-part series entitled *Growing Up Baboon* that featured the work of Rita Miljo and the staff of C.A.R.E. (Center for Animal Rehabilitation and Education). For almost twenty years, Rita had been devoting herself single-mindedly to the adoption, care, and release of orphaned infant chacma baboons at this Center she, along with a nine-year-old female baboon named Bobby founded in 1989.

• • •

Though this is a story about baboons, not just about Rita Miljo, it must remain, at least for a while, with her, for it is with her that this all began. I first learned about Rita, as I just said, on television. Now Rita isn't a baboon, rest assured—though I would hardly be surprised to learn that, in a previous life, she was one. Rita is a nearly eighty-year-old woman with the spirit of a sixteen-year-old girl and the force of a tornado. And she is not terribly fond of us humans. But she *does* love baboons.

There was something about Rita Miljo, from the first time I saw her face and heard her voice that immediately reminded me of a composite of the German filmmaker Leni Riefenstahl—who, among other things, made propaganda films for Hitler—and the American painter Georgia O'Keefe: It was the aging beauty and the deep character of her face, the sense of an iron will coupled with a fierce determination and fearlessness, her deeply *sabra*-like personality—that renowned Israeli desert cactus, after which native-born Israeli women are named, that is so sharp and prickly on the outside, so sweet and juicy within. Somewhere beneath that tough and intimidating exterior, I sensed, lay a certain sweetness.

I knew from the outset that here was a woman I wanted to meet and get to know. And then, once I came to know her, I realized that, for the first time in my life as a writer, it was not myself, but someone *else*, I wanted to write a book about. This unique and courageous woman—her work, her history, her world, her way of looking at life—had a story that deserved and needed to be shared with a wider audience.

When I saw Rita and her baboons that night on *Animal Planet* and realized that maybe I, too, could go to Phalaborwa and work "hands on" with these primates, I simply picked up the phone and dialed Rita's number. Hardly five months later, a small plane carrying me from Johannesburg to South Africa's northernmost Limpopo Province touched down in at Phalaborwa's diminutive, one-runway airport.

Rita had created her Center on a fifty-acre patch of African bush she had bought in South Africa's Limpopo Province. The rest, as the baboons might say if they could, is history . . . or, rather, *her* and *their* story. And it was this that brought us together, on many South African winter evenings, in a single room, a meeting of two people that could only have been caused by one of Rita's favorite expressions: "human error."

. . .

So what can be said, in a nutshell, about the life of Rita Miljo? That she was born Rita Neumann to a middle-class family on the outskirts of Königsberg in the far northeastern corner of Germany near the Russian border, in 1931; that, as a young girl, she joined and served in the Hitler Youth; that, even as an adolescent, when she left her family to work in Hamburg's renowned Hagenbeck Zoo, she felt a deep identification with animals; that she married a young German engineer by the name of Lothar Simon, with whom she emigrated to South Africa, in 1953; that, while in Africa, she learned to fly planes,), lay bricks, and build houses; that she consumed everything about baboons and other African animals a mere lay person—or even a so-called expert—could possibly hope to know; that she bought a piece of wilderness along the Oliphants River in 1963; and that her husband and seventeen-year-old daughter died tragically in a small plane crash in 1972.

Eight years after the accident, during her brief second marriage to Piet Miljo, an Afrikaner, Rita made what might be regarded as the transforming acquaintance of her life. While traveling in northern Namibia, she encountered a neglected and abused female chacma baboon named Bobby. (In fact, all anonymous baboons in South Africa were dubbed Bobby, after the Afrikaans name for the species, *bobbejaan*.) Bobby was being kept, poorly, as a mascot at a military encampment. In defiance of the requirement for permits, Rita took Bobby home, and a bond between species was forged.

In 1989, along with Bennett Serane a native South African, Rita founded C.A.R.E., and her fifty acres of bush became a refuge where injured wild animals—various birds, reptiles, and small mammals, initially—were treated and released.

As increasing numbers of injured or abused chacma baboons were brought in, mostly orphaned babies, the Center began to specialize. Agricultural lands had encroached on the baboons' natural habitat, and wherever crops were threatened, farmers had the right to shoot the offending "vermin." Poaching, poisoning, illegal trade in pets and experimental animals, as well as environmental hazards (natural or otherwise) left behind orphaned and injured baboons in need of C.A.R.E.

But these are mere facts, mere biographical data, and—while they tell you something about Rita Miljo's spirit of fearlessness, adventure, and commitment—they tell you, in the end, very little about the person I came to know some twenty-five kilometers from the copper mining town of Phalaborwa in South Africa in May of 2007. Because, as always, the person is more interesting, more elusive of true knowing, more complex, than the biography can ever be.

So, after a few days as a C.A.R.E. volunteer, when I began to sense that Rita, a bit grudgingly, had taken a liking to me, I proposed a deal: I would come to Rita's house—consisting, essentially, of a single overstuffed living room that also serves as the Center's office, and an upstairs loft, where Rita sleeps—every night after supper. We'd have a glass of wine, and then we would discuss whatever subject *I* chose for the evening's agenda. "Agreed?"

"Oh, Michael," Rita began in a world-and-Michael-weary way, "all right, if we must. . . . Agreed."

• • •

Rita Miljo is also not a woman who shies away from controversy, especially when it comes to saving baboons. The task she has undertaken is rendered even more formidable by the fact that baboons, even among animal lovers, are hardly at the top of the list of best-loved primates. For one, they are not readily amenable to being dressed in overalls or *Lederhosen* and paraded onto the late-night TV shows. Secondly, when they become full-grown, they develop not the relatively flat, universally beloved and human-like faces of chimpanzees and bonobos, but instead a more elongated and snout-like visage that is reminiscent of a dog. And thirdly they are ferociously resourceful and smart—so much so that, yes, they can easily become a pest to anyone whose house, car, refrigerator, or garden they put their minds to getting into.

At times, Rita's stubborn determination to give voice to these often-detested primates has landed her, not only on the dark side of her neighbors' indulgences, but in court. As in September of 2005, when she was charged by the South African authorities with illegally transporting an injured baboon from Mpumalanga Park to Limpopo Province without the requisite permit.

In true Gandhiesque fashion, Rita readily admitted to having violated the law, but claimed she had done so out of necessity, or else the baboon would have been neglected or killed due to deliberate delays in the Mpumalanga Park Board's permit-issuing procedures. She testified that, on a previous occasion, a baboon she had tried to rescue *had* died because of similar delays in issuing the required permit.

Declaring that "the court is sure that what she [Rita] did was what an ordinary citizen in the circumstances would have done," the Mpumalanga magistrate, in a decision hailed by animal rights activists everywhere, including C.A.R.E.'s main funder, the IFAW (International Fund for Animal Welfare), ruled that the Park's obstructive permit policies were hampering the work of a world-renowned baboon rehabilitation specialist. What's more, the magistrate ruled, conservation officials had displayed "a contemptuous attitude" toward Rita and her work that had caused considerable delays, sometimes lasting years, in issuing her the permits she needed to carry out her work.

"The life of the animal was under threat and needed to be saved," Helen Dagut, IFAW's Southern Africa campaign manager, said at the time. "It was necessary for [Rita] to break the law to do this and the magistrate acknowledged it."

. . .

There is, in the end, one ultimate goal of all this mothering, caging, feeding, transferring, and juggling of infant and young baboons at C.A.R.E.: namely, freedom. In the nearly twenty years of the Center's existence, some dozen baboon "troops" numbering roughly 250 baboons have been released into sites all around South Africa—a process so time-consuming and complex it could easily occupy five times Rita's roughly ten-member staff. Not only must the appropriate release sites be located, permits applied for, the individual troops prepared for their release and transported, and at least two staff members dispensed to the release site for up to five months to make certain the baboons have acclimated and are able to successfully forage for food on their own, but also follow-up by Rita and her staff to check on the troop's welfare can continue, literally, for years—and sometimes with discouraging results.

In the case of the troop that was at the release site during my stay, that same troop had already been released once before—five years back, to be precise, at which time they had survived for four years in the wild. But then, as baboon luck would have it, the farmer on whose land they had been released died, and his son, who had inherited the land, threatened to poison the troop if C.A.R.E. didn't come and get them. Rita and her assistant Lee Dekker then went back to the site during the night and recaptured the remainder of the troop—a process that involved constructing an A-frame, filling it with food, and trapping the alpha males in cages first, followed by the mature females, until finally only the young, more easy to capture, were left. They then brought them back to C.A.R.E. and had to begin the whole release process over again.

"You know," Rita says when I posed the usual naïve question, 'Why baboons?,' "they are the last creatures under the sun that nobody cares about. That's why. When I first started, everybody said to me, 'With all that energy you've got, why don't you look after rhinos or cheetahs,' or whatever else it was they cared about? And I always answered, 'Because these guys need me.'"

. . .

These guys *do* need her, as I am soon to discover. The morning I arrive in Phalaborwa from Johannesburg, I am picked up at the airport, as are most volunteers, by thirty-eight-year-old Center Manager Lee Dekker, a Pretoria native who has been at the Center full-time for over two years. Lee, I was forewarned, usually arrives at the airport carrying one of the infant baboons she's foster-mothering in a shawl tied around her waist. But today she has only a baboon-imprinted T-shirt and a trademark scratch on her left cheek (a rite of passage I am soon to carry with me as well). She's had to leave her baby, Suzie, at C.A.R.E. while doing the weekly food shopping for the volunteers in town. Lee is a highly energetic, affable woman who exudes an air of focused commitment and utter competence. "The situation for wildlife in Africa is essentially hopeless," she tells me en route, "but we keep trying."

We stop at the Phalaborwa Mall to do the shopping before making our way along the Mica Road for some twenty-five kilometers to the signpost marked Grietjie that leads down the badly corrugated and boulder-strewn road leading to C.A.R.E. As we drive along the upper bank of the crocodile- and hippo-filled Oliphants River, we come to a memorial grave marker bearing a wreath. Beneath it rests the remains of a neighbor's son who, several years earlier, had had a few too many beers with friends before, oblivious to what awaited him within its murky waters, jumping into the river for a swim.

"Don't ever walk along the river bank by yourself at night," Lee warns me, "and, for God's sake, don't *ever* go swimming in it. We don't want to put one of these up for you."

. . .

When we arrive at the C.A.R.E. headquarters, wild baboons emerge from every direction to make a desperate grab for the groceries in the back of Lee's truck. We remove the temptation at what seems to be great peril, and then Lee shows me to my room. I've been assigned the "honeymoon suite" among the volunteers' quarters, being perched, as it is, directly adjacent to the C.A.R.E. office and Rita's "private" quarters (shared, of course, with dozens of infant baboons), and featuring that rarest of volunteer amenities—a shower of its own. (My having spoken German with Rita on the phone when I first called, and having introduced myself as a writer, must have paid off.)

"I hope you don't mind the company of creepy crawly things," Lee comments with a smile as she places my bag beside the mosquito-net-covered bed. "You'll have plenty of that."

"Company," I quickly discover, is a piece of radical understatement. When I pull open the battered dresser drawer to unpack my things, an armada of cockroaches so vast and so large they seem like something out of Camus' *The Plague,* pours out of every corner and streams onto the floor of my cottage, heading for cover. I grew up with plenty of cockroaches in the ghetto of Washington Heights, but these are of a size and seeming ferocity that takes me right back to a horror movie from my childhood starring Boris Karlov, *The Tingler.*

Hardly have I recovered from this first outpouring of hospitality from the African insect world than—when I climb onto the bed to straighten a supermarket-quality print of the African bush that hangs directly above it—a flotilla of spiders of every imaginable size and shape invades my space from each corner of the frame, scattering every which way throughout the room and into my bed. I quickly gaze at the return date on my airline ticket: *five weeks from today*. I gulp, take a deep breath, and finish unpacking.

Just after I have had a chance to finish unpacking and, so to speak, "settle in," Rita takes me for a walk down to the river, where the wild troop is serenely engaged in their late-afternoon grooming. "The perfect peace emblem," noted baboon researcher Shirley Strum has written in her respected study, *Almost Human*, "should not be a dove, but two baboons grooming." And, watching the peaceful near-dusk scene unfolding before us, I can begin to appreciate what she means.

Rita points out a huge crocodile sunbathing on the other side of the river, then a group of bush-bucks beneath the trees ahead of us, and then, in rapid succession, a number of animal tracks that are right at our feet—hippo, monitor lizard, water buffalo, water buck. "You can live here very peaceably with the animals," Rita says as we walk along the river, "if you just learn to respect them and keep out of their way."

There seems to be nothing this woman doesn't know about the animal world, and, as we walk, she regales me with various stories of the twenty-odd other individuals and families who are co-owners of plots within the bush reserve.

There was the Brit across the river, for example, who originally brought his place for three million Rand, and then sold off eighty-five shares for a million Rand each. When he died of a heart attack on a boat trip at age thirty-five, "I wanted to throw a party," Rita says without apology. This is not, I find out very quickly, a woman who pulls her punches. "The one thing I learned from Hitler," she confesses, "was how to fight, and win."

It is a lesson she has made good use of here in the South African bush, often against great odds.

· · ·

Like so many of the other volunteers who come to C.A.R.E., I saw that the confluence of my motives and what the program depicted was a perfect match. "I had always been interested in primates," Kim, a volunteer from California who was making her fourth visit in less than two years, told me, "and I wanted to do something 'ands on,'" a sentiment that echoes my own feelings more or less exactly.

The volunteers, like a baboon troop itself, are rather a motley crew. Along with Elena and Zurika, two young women from Italy and South Africa, respectively, who are basically in charge of the volunteers, there's Jacob and Doris, a transplanted South Dakotan and Canadian couple who had been living and working in California for several years, and who had just retired from their careers, sold their house and all their belongings, and are completing the first year of what is to be a two-and-a-half year 'round-the-world trip. There's also Kim, a former real estate investment manager from Laguna Beach, California, who is here for the fourth time in less than two years.

I soon notice a certain parallel between the baboon troops and the "troop" of volunteers: Each time a new member arrives, there's a sometimes subtle, but nonetheless pronounced, shift in group dynamics—the token males jockeying for position, the females dominating the whole show.

As Lee so aptly puts it one night when I comment on the latter, "They always said it was a man's world. But the baboons have shown us it isn't so."

There's also Alex, president of the Swedish Association for Gay, Lesbian, and Transgendered Rights, who has just attended an international conference in Johannesburg and is only spending a week; Diana, from the Netherlands, a secretary who wants to change her life and work full-time with primates; and Mackenzie, a veterinarian's assistant from Phoenix who has contracted a terrible intestinal virus after only a week here, and is in the hospital in nearby Zaneen when I arrive.

Emma is a twenty-year-old primate-biology major from Columbia who already knows just how she will spend her life: more or less just like we are now … or, at least, in some related capacity. Kryzstof, a Polish veterinary student from Breslau, arrived after I did. Filled with zeal and good intentions (and with a seeming ease with the animals that I envy), Kryzstof came from a nearby private game lodge where he'd been volunteering. But on his second night, after his parents asked him on the phone whether one can get AIDS from the baboons (the answer is "no"), he got so freaked out at the prospect that he decided to leave.

"And *that* boy," says Rita with a sense of bemused wonderment, "wants to become a veterinarian!"

"Piss and poop," the other male volunteer, Jacob, says to me during my first night's supper, "is the story of working with primates." And piss and poop it is. *"Your clothing will get 'peed and pooed' on and you may not want to wear it again later, so don't bring your best!"* is how the *Volunteer Information Guide* sent to volunteers prior to their departure put it. A textbook example of truth in advertising!

⁕ ⁕ ⁕

What a volunteer actually has his or her "hands on" in coming to C.A.R.E., almost from the moment Lee's truck pulls past the Center's hardly conspicuous nameplate, are baboons—wild baboons, caged baboons, and baboons eagerly jumping on the back of the truck to help themselves to the victuals before Lee can stop, pick up a couple of stones to frighten them off, and pull in behind the fenced gate.

May mornings at C.A.R.E., at least for me, begin at precisely 5:57 a.m. They begin, to be more precise, with a crescendo-like sound akin to the falling of immense hailstones on my room's corrugated aluminum roof—the sound of mostly adult baboons descending from their sleeping perches in the sycamore tree just below—coupled with a fervent chorus of *wa-hoos* and copulation cries as the day begins, with its mixed cacophony of dangers, hungers, and lusts.

What you learn in your first few minutes at C.A.R.E. is that there are actually *two* troops of baboons in residence—the wild troop, numbering somewhere around one hundred twenty and affectionately named the *Longtits* by Rita for reasons that take little time to become apparent; and the caged troop, whose cages, or *hoks* (in Afrikaans), are dispersed all over the property, and who usually number between three and five hundred. The wild baboons moved in shortly after the mid 1980s when Rita, her five ridgebacks, and Bobby first arrived in Rita's tiny caravan.

· · ·

In the wild, a female baboon weans her baby at between six and eight months, a process that takes place in essentially four stages. During the first week or so, the mother holds the baby tightly against her body and forages on three legs. In the second phase, when the baby's arms are stronger, it hangs underneath the mother, suckling on a nipple. Next comes the jockey position, when the baby sits on its mother's rump and leans against her tail as she feeds; and, finally, the walking phase, wherein the infant begins to do its own foraging and prepares for independence.

C.A.R.E.'s weaning process, however, being a somewhat 'unnatural' variation, is also somewhat more complex. It begins, for the first month or two, with what is called "24/7," and means just that: The infant spends twenty-four hours a day—including time in the shower (and, yes, in case you're truly interested, on the toilet)—either tied around its human volunteer surrogate mother's waist in a shawl, or in her arms. When Rita, the surrogate mother, and the staff think the infant is ready, it is moved to the nursery with the other infants for several hours a day, returning to sleep with the mother at night. This phase slowly morphs into the next—usually at around two months— when the infant grows comfortable with spending the entire day in the nursery, and only nights with its mother.

During the final phase, during which the little babies seem most unhappy, the infant continues to sleep in the surrogate mother's room at night, but in a small cage. This prepares it for its real "move" into post-infancy, when it will begin to sleep along with the other infants—*and*, of course, their stuffed animals—in cages set up in Rita's bathroom in the main house.

. . .

It's also a hierarchical world, this world of baboons, and though Rita, to be sure, loves all her children, there are certain hierarchies within her affections—or, at least, her discipline—as well. Scruffy, for example, a patient and persistent mid-sized female, is—much to the dismay of the staff!—granted the rare privilege of entrance to Rita's freezer, an opportunity she makes the most of, not only by helping herself to the food inside, but frequently by toppling the barrel of corn Rita keeps for the wild troop and spreading the kernels on the kitchen floor. Several other members of the wild troop have developed the habit of waiting at what Rita calls her "take-out window," for the occasional banana, apple or tomato she obligingly tosses their way.

The most special treatment of all, however, is reserved for Tripsy, an aged and infirm female and the oldest member of the wild troop, who receives, hand-delivered, a pitcher of milk and several raw eggs every morning. Along with the aged and infirm, there are also special feedings for a pair of suricates (also known as meerkats), a squirrel, a lamed warthog, and—occasionally, when Rita, in near secrecy, makes her way down the hill late at night with the day's leftovers of meat and bones—the jackals.

"They are all God's creatures," says Rita, invoking a deity she doesn't seem to actually believe in. "Who are we to create a hierarchy among them?"

. . .

Within the genus of *Papio*, or savanna, baboons, of which Limpopo's chacma baboons are members, there are now considered to be nine subspecies. "Isn't it funny," Rita says to me, "how God could have had enough foresight to make South Africa have nine provinces [during Apartheid there were four], when we also have nine sub-species of baboon!"

There is also no small irony in that fact that someone like Rita, who grew up under the racial laws of Hitler's Germany, would have been confronted not only by South Africa's Apartheid system, but also by what she calls its *Rassenmischung* (racial mixing) laws regarding the classification of baboons. Until just a few years ago, these laws made it impossible for C.A.R.E. to obtain the required permits to release its baboons to sites occupied by other subspecies, as such mixing of subspecies was not allowed. But, in no small part due to the persistent efforts of C.A.R.E. and the I.L.A.W., these laws are no longer on the books. Nonetheless, with the infant mortality rate among baboons often as high as seventy or eighty percent and human settlements increasingly encroaching on what was once the baboons' natural habitat, baboon troops have now vanished from roughly eighty percent of the area of South Africa's Cape Peninsula.

It's precisely this trend that Rita and the staff of C.A.R.E. have set out to reverse. But even the pre-release procedure is fraught with complexity: First, one of the staff members—either release manager Steve Munro (now C.A.R.E.'s director) or former release manager Davie van der Merwe must bond tightly with the troop's alpha males. Then, a sleeping tree must be located as a central gathering place. The release managers, who sleep at the site in tents, slowly but surely lead the baboons to water, fruiting trees, and other foraging sites until the males are able to find those places themselves. This last phase usually lasts about five months, during which time at least one of them remains constantly with the troop.

In capitalist parlance, this long investment in releasing a troop of between fifteen and twenty-two baboons is bad economics indeed— as was Rita and my driving 120 kilometers to Zaneen, a four-hour-long round trip, just to pick up a shipment of 500 pounds of kernel corn, mostly for the wild troop. "Inefficiencies" such as these—or such as Lee's twelve-hour round-trip drive to Johannesburg to pick up three new baboons—pervade C.A.R.E.'s work. But the investment here, as Rita is quick to point out, has nothing to do with such calculations: It costs some $15,000 a month just to keep the Center going, and the only cost-benefit analysis that ever takes place is how it will be humanly possible to save, and release, the baboons.

"People turn everything on this bloody planet into money making," she told me one night. "It's the biggest mistake that humankind could have made. . . . It's sick. It isn't right, and it will, in the long run, ruin us."

• • •

One of the most amazing things, I quickly discover, about baboons is their acuity of vision. I witness two vivid examples of this early in my stay—first during the morning "wake-up" turbulence when, hoping to tape some of the *wa-hooing* and copulation cries to play for my wife and son back in France, I placed my small pocket tape recorder on top of a beam just inside the wire mesh separating me from the troop. Within less than five seconds, the baboons had spotted it and knocked it to the ground, trying to steal it!

Almost the same thing happened hardly an hour later when, bending down to tie my shoe, I placed a copy of *The History of South Africa* I am reading between the metal door and the doorjamb of the volunteers' lodge. Before I could even begin to tie a knot, a young baboon was seated on the roof eagerly "reading" my book, soon (perhaps out of boredom!) to be torn to shreds. This is a lesson I was to gather evidence of repeatedly during my stay: One of the main reasons many people don't love baboons is that they are constantly showing us how much cleverer they are than we are.

Two other remarkable qualities about baboons are their ability to tolerate pain—a baboon can be dragged, pulled, bitten and clawed so much in the course of the average day, even by its own family, that its very survival, much less its prospering, seems a near miracle—and their almost incredible healing powers. One of the smalls, Zefferelli, for example, had several bones in his right arm fractured when a member of the wild troop attempted to pull him right through the cage. Within an hour, after Lee and Rita had placed a cast on the arm, he was back in the cage, acting as if nothing had ever gone wrong. Virtually the same was true of Diva, Kim's not-even-month-old little baby, who had her arm broken in a similar fashion. Though she had to be taken into Phalaborwa for antibiotics and a cast, Diva, too, was back in her pouch astride Kim by the end of the day.

The frequent hostility between man and baboon—fueled mostly by ignorance as to what baboons truly are and aren't—has produced a series of myths and utter fabrications that have endured for hundreds of years. Baboons play an important role in traditional African beliefs. The Khoisian people, who originally occupied much of sub-equatorial Africa as hunter-gatherers, believed that baboons, along with snakes, were people in an altered state of consciousness. Other African tribes believed baboons, as well as lions, to be capable of mysterious powers, powers that in African society could normally be attained only by shamans and witchdoctors.

In South Africa itself, however, the present-day fate of baboons has been far less mystical. People once received money for a baboon scalp and tail; and, until quite recently, baboons could be shot on sight by farmers and others as mere "vermin." Contemporary folk tales, in Africa and elsewhere, freely portray baboons as stupid and lazy—In most cultures, including our own, "You stupid baboon" is still a common insult.

• • •

Mine is a fairly typical volunteers' schedule: give bottles from 11:00–12:00 (some six hundred and fifty bottles of powdered milk are distributed to the various *hoks* daily) with mediums (between eight months and a year old) from 1:00–2:00, smalls (between four and eight months) from 2:00–3:00, and the nursery from 4:00–5:00. At around 5:30—it is now South African winter and getting dark early—all three groups of babies will be brought into Rita's house and the adjoining bathroom and kitchen to spend the night.

Baboon society is a profoundly gender-oriented world, complete with remarkable gender-detecting genes. This I quickly discover the first morning I enter the nursery, or kindergarten, *hok* where the mostly two-to-four-month-old infants spend the large part of their day. These infants *know* I am both a stranger and a man, and, from the moment I step into the cage, they beat a hasty and rather noisy retreat into Elena's already baboon-filled arms. "They just need to get used to you," she consoles me, "and they're terribly afraid of men at first."

The fact that these young baboons are terribly afraid of new men had already been graphically illustrated to me that very morning in the mediums' cage, where I have my first exposure to the baboon cry for "help!" and to being "mobbed" by a group of frightened baboons. There are seventeen roughly one-year-old baboons in the mediums' cage—ten females and seven males—and Dennis, with whom I will eventually develop my deepest and most complicated relationship, quickly decides I am a threat.

Just when I think I am beginning to develop a rather friendly, if cautious, relationship with him in particular, something I do—perhaps an inadvertently raised eyebrow or a set of teeth too conspicuously revealed—seems to trigger his anxiety and he immediately issues a high-pitched warning cry. Suddenly, hierarchical competitiveness be damned, *all seventeen* of the mediums, teeth bared, make their way at my calves, my arms, my thighs, my waist.

"Ah Ah Ah!!" cries Zurika, mimicking the baboon cry for *Get away!* or *Cut that out!*, yanking several of the playful young tykes off me by their arms, legs, scruff of the neck, ears, and tails. (Baboons, as I mentioned, have an extraordinary capacity for pain. Acts that would easily

land you in jail, if not a psychiatric ward, if inflicted on your own child aren't even a slap on the wrist when dealing with an infant baboon.)

That night, as I stand talking to Rita, there's a sudden hubbub among the staff, signaling what I will come to realize are one of C.A.R.E.'s almost daily series of small and large emergencies. In this instance, one of the babies has escaped from one of the *hoks* outside, and Lee and Senior Animal Keeper Bennett Serane run off to retrieve it.

"Human error," says Rita, mouthing one of her favorite shorthand sentiments. "Human error."

• • •

Once you have picked, cajoled, lifted, and forced enough of the little guys and girls from your head, thighs, shoulders, and waist to take a seat on one of the plastic food crates provided for that purpose, you must wrestle with the first of many challenges about to confront you: How to tell the Dennises, Kimberlys, Tortillas, Yoshis, Judys and Jaggers apart. It's a bit like entering a maternity ward and being asked to tell the newborns apart. But everyone *else* seems easily able to do it. Why not me?

The male/female bit, of course, is easy enough. If you can't stop them moving long enough to spot a penis, or the lack of one, there's a simple way: In the males, the *callosities*, or buttocks, are fused below the anus; in the females, they are conveniently separated to make room for the sexual organs. And then, slowly but surely, you become aware of the subtle differences and demarcations: Kimberly has rough, thick gray fur and—with the exception of Sunamu, the alpha female—is the largest of the troop; Icarus has several white scar markings on his left cheek; Maggie, along with the fact that she is hardly ever separated from her brother Dennis, is missing a tail; Sunamu has smooth streaked fur on her back; Jagger is yellowish brown and, by comparison to the others, rather emaciated; Cory is the one practicing masturbation on your left knee. After a few weeks of this, I can almost swear that my eyes are becoming as focused and discriminating as the baboons'!

One of the first things I need to learn in my relationship with my new charges is baboon language: lip-smacking, grunting, warning calls, laughing sounds, mating cries—the emotional range is rather astonishing. I soon become acquainted with the warning cry through harsh experience: namely, when it issues from the lips of Dennis among the mediums and Peter among the smalls as a call to mob me. In the meantime, I arduously practice my lip smacking—the ultimate accompaniment (along with ears pulled back against the head) to the 'come-hither' face of proffered friendship—in front of the mirror. I'm all too aware that mine more accurately resembles a forlorn lover blowing kisses than a baboon trying to be friends, but, after all, I'm only a beginner.

As for the wild troop, there are things to be learned there too: For one, it isn't wise, especially for a man, to make direct eye contact with one of the large males: It's seen as a challenge, and can provoke an unwelcome response. Another is that, when males are copulating or busy grooming a prospective mate, it's best to keep a certain distance—or, at least, not interrupt the proceedings. Picking up a rock— picking it up, not necessarily throwing it!—is sure to intimidate even the large males (who are merely likely to give you a push as a way of letting you know who's boss), but it isn't always wise to do so, I quickly discover when one of the other volunteers, Angela, picks one up right in front of a copulating couple, only to be rewarded by a large shove from the male.

• • •

You can pick your friends and you can pick your nose, but you can't pick your friend's nose was a popular saying when I was a kid growing up in Manhattan, but it certainly isn't the prevailing ethos here. Maggie, whose tail has been bitten off in a fight, is clearly becoming my friend—at least judging from the ardor with which she preens and grooms me. She is also not at all averse to picking at my nose, or my ears, my eyelids, my lips and gums and any other protrusion or orifice she can reach.

In the nursery on the late afternoon of my first full day as a volunteer I meet Shanti, a two-month-old female who greets me with a flattering, and utterly archetypal, gesture: the presentation of her *derrière*. The presenting of the female buttocks, in the hope that the honoree will comply by scratching it, is a gesture of incipient friendship and interest. (It can also have other functions among older baboons, such as expressing a desire for grooming or copulation, or surrender after a fight.) So, obediently, I scratch. Shanti, temporarily satisfied, scoots off playfully into the arms of Elena, then returns for more.

Shanti's story—heartbreaking but not uncharacteristic of orphans who had the good fortune to fall into C.A.R.E.'s hands—is that the man who previously owned her had nourished her largely on *alcohol*, a substance infant baboons will ingest all too readily. Within days of her arrival at C.A.R.E., it became clear that poor little Shanti was going through detox. Originally Lee's baby, he seems to take a liking to Jacob, who agrees to take on the rather unique status of being a male "stepmother."

Nor is this to be the last of Shanti's medical adventures: When, after discovering a bleeding polyp inside her, Lee administers a sedative that is probably too much for her damaged liver, Shanti goes into shock. Thinking her little infant is dying, Lee bursts into tears. But then, on the way to the vet, the heroic little creature revives, and, by evening, is back to normal, sitting at the dinner table in Jacob's pouch along with the other volunteers.

• • •

It's with Dennis that I develop the most complicated, and at times perplexing, relationship. Dennis is the youngster whose warning cries first led to my being mobbed by the troop. All I need to do is consult the various scratch and bite marks on my arms and legs to be reminded of the occasion. During my first few sessions with the mediums, he repeatedly comes to me for comfort, but, when I apparently don't give him enough, or the right kind, immediately begins biting me, or crying out for help.

Dennis is also beginning to rely on me for protection from Sunamu and the other larger members of his troop. Along with his devoted sister Maggie, my hairdresser, he now spends most of the time when I am in the mediums' cage grunting and vocalizing in my arms, to whose comfort he frequently retreats, grooming my arms, my chest and, finally, my head to calm himself.

Days later, however, Dennis twice initiates yet another mobbing of me. This is interesting, because one tends to project the 'human' expectation of gratitude—after all, who's been protecting and cuddling him continuously the past several days?—onto the baboon world, where it hardly applies. Fact is, Dennis is very low, perhaps lowest, within the troop hierarchy, and, as Rita says, those of low rank will often "switch sides" against a common enemy (me!) as a way of trying to ally themselves with their more powerful troop mates.

I decide to adopt a new strategy with Dennis, which actually seems to work: I studiously avoid any eye contact with him, no matter how hard he seems to be trying to meet my gaze. I sense he is just waiting for my eyes to meet his to give out the *help!* cry and have the others come mob me, but I'm not buying. I also let Sunamu and the others beat up on him at will and pull him off my lap. This seems to be working: No trouble the first day, at least.

On my second day entirely alone with mediums (volunteers, especially males, are never left alone in the baboon cages until the baboons have come to know, and feel comfortable, with them), Dennis approaches me relentlessly for comfort, yelping his little *help!* cry until I squeeze him to my chest and stroke his head. It's astonishing—and in many ways quite moving—to realize that these baboons are actually beginning to *know*, and to trust, me. We seem light years away from the mawlings and mobbings of my first several days.

As the days march on, Dennis, in fact, is so sure of my protectiveness that he feels confident enough to attack Sunamu, the alpha female and troop leader, who does reverse somersaults between my legs chasing him. Dennis and his sister Maggie, with whom, arm in arm, he occasionally does a Fred Astaire and Ginger Rodgers soft shoe around the cage, grooms my chest hairs, while Sabrina and Kariba groom those on my legs. Even Sunamu takes a turn at grooming me, which suggests that, finally, I had *really* made it!

Dennis's behavior, on the other hand, remains strange and unpredictable. A real momma's boy, he come to me perpetually for comfort, occasionally even risking a small act of aggression at one of the other baboons, and then immediately running back into my arms screeching and squealing. Yet eye contact with me seems to frighten him, and, whenever I look at him or try to lip smack him, he takes off screaming! He does the same at bedtime, when I try to take him inside.

The smalls, slowly but surely, are beginning to take a liking to me as well—though how that 'liking' manifests itself isn't always what one might hope for. Komoti, for example, begins manically grooming my chest—a 'grooming' that includes pulling on my chest hairs as well. Zefferelli, on the other hand, chooses the approach/avoidance method: Bandaged arm and all, he performs an interesting dance, usually on my left knee, mounting my knee, sitting down, opening his arms wide, lip smacking me, and then taking off on a frantic run in the other direction, sometimes pausing just to pee on my leg before departing. Flirtation? Game? Whatever it is he may want from me, his behavior reminds me of something I'd read in Shirley Strum's *Almost Human* before coming to C.A.R.E.:

I have observed baboons when meeting for the first time, advancing and retreating . . . a slow respectful means of getting to know each other. Sometimes their language is so indirect that it is difficult to detect at all and in human terms it appears as if they were ignoring each other when in fact they are merely acknowledging the other's personal boundaries.

So there you have it: Zeferelli is merely trying to get to know me, just offering his respect.

. . .

It's hard to say whether a troop of seventeen eight-to-twelve-month-old baboons having been nicer to one on any one day than the day before substantially raises one's spirits is a sign of having risen, or fallen, within one's own not-so-humble species, but—risen or fallen—that's how I am starting to feel. The mediums seem actively *happy* to see me, with Kimberly jumping down on me at least a dozen times from the wooden post above and lying playfully in my lap, and Tortilla and Sabrina madly vying for Maggie's hairdresser role.

My Dennis strategy, too, seems to be working: He's constantly trying to make eye contact, first from my lap and then from various vantage points around the cage, but I steadfastly hold to my resolve: stroking and lap dancing are fine; eye contact, no.

In the nursery (which is all girls) later that afternoon, Shakira continues presenting her pinkish little bottom, which I obediently scratch, while Petri and Maya—what a compliment!—carouse on my lap. Even Emilia and Thandi flirt with me from the safety of Elena's lap, while Shanti does a frantic little dance between us and Willow, Zurika's baby, peeks curiously out from beneath her blanket. This, in the world of a new "alpha male" being introduced to a troop of infant females, is real progress.

. . .

The next day, which begins as usual with a crescendo of *wa-hooing* from above, coupled with the occasional copulation cry and the hailstone-like descent of baboon feet from the trees and cages above, proves to be an eventful one: That morning, as I am sitting among the mediums with Elena, and just after Elle, one of the caged troop, has tried to steal baby Suzi from Elena's arms and Sabrina, another member of the troop, steals the baby blanket, I see Bennett, Rita, and Lee running up to Area 1, where one of the adult baboons has been found dead. Elena runs out to help and for the first time I find myself alone with the mediums, hoping Dennis wouldn't instigate another mobbing. When a baby cobra drops from the blanket containing the dead baboon, Rita thinks, at first, that a cobra bite has done the damage. ("The babies," she says as she walks past, "have enough poison in them to kill too.") But once the dead baboon is brought inside, his purplish-black tongue reveals he has died of asphyxiation, the product of a black mamba bite, the deadliest bite of all.

There have now, in the brief time since my arrival, been three baboon deaths (two from snakebite, one from tetanus), along with the three mawlings—of Diva, Zefferelli, and Thandi. Each day, I am soon to realize, brings its little panoply of small and large emergencies: illnesses, accidents, deaths, injuries, escapes, fights.

The time alone with the mediums passes, gratefully, without incident, and, later that day in the nursery, it's only Petri who takes an interest in engaging me, with an occasional tentative foray on Thandi's part. It occurs to me as I sit there that human-baboon interactions can, at least at the outset, be a one-way street: It's up to us humans, somehow, to enter the world of baboon-ness in order successfully to interact with them . . . waiting for *them* to act like *us* is utterly futile.

• • •

As I begin spending more and more time alone with the mediums, it's not only Dennis and Maggie with whom I seem to be making progress. Sabrina and Karima also begin relentlessly grooming me; Kimberly, apparently eager to show off her gymnastic skills, delivers a flying drop kick to my left eye on one occasion, turning it bright pink, as she catapults off a beam; even Sunamu begins presenting her lovely pink behind.

"You're in here all by yourself?" Rita says with a smile as she walks past.

"I sure am. See . . . I'm not as frightened as you thought."

"You are *very very* brave," the boss reassures me.

Baboons are relentlessly curious, and one of the great pleasures of spending time with the mediums is watching them—whenever, for example, a group of young baby warthogs walks by or there is any commotion in front of Rita's door—line up against the front of the cage, noses pressed against the fence like a bunch of children lining up to watch a Thanksgiving Day parade.

Among the smalls, Johnny, Brutus and Komoti are also getting used to me, and, in the nursery, Lee's baby, Suzie, keeps making tentative approaches, then retreating. Shakira, Petri and, to a lesser extent, Thandi, now all seem more relaxed in my company. I am also starting to deliver afternoon milk to the older adolescents in Star *Hok*, who seem to like the game of having me chase them around the cage to retrieve the baby bottles and nipples.

That evening, on my pre-sundown walk along the beach, I see one of the wild troop females carrying what looks like a black dishrag, hanging limply from her hand. Training my binoculars on her, I realize that it is a dead baby she's been carrying around, a fact Rita confirms later that evening. "The mother," she explains to me, "was too young to know how to care for it," a situation I realize also sometimes has its human counterpart.

* * *

The truth is that, by the end of my second week at C.A.R.E., I've begun to feel a bit baboony myself. I'm actually beginning to enjoy this sitting around being groomed, presented to, and lip-smacked. What's more, it isn't a bad life being the alpha male. I get a lot of attention! Somebody up there on my head—Tortilla? Sabrina?—seems to have fallen absolutely in love with me. She madly grooms my hair and my eyes, then moves on to my chest, along with periodic yanks on my chest hairs, and methodically chews off all three buttons on my shirt. But all in all it's a good life here in the cage—calming, tranquil, even meditative.

"I was in baby *hok*," volunteer Kim Sobakk recalls to me one day over lunch, "and there were seven or eight babies in there with me, and I leaned back and they were all lying on my chest and the sun was coming through the trees, and it was the most magical moment I can ever remember." I am beginning to understand what she meant.

Even Sunamu actually *twice* engages me in long, intimate grooming sessions. She now seems much less after Dennis. While Stella and Judy, two of the more yellowish females, have taken up residence on my left knee, opposite Dennis and Maggie. Then, also, there are lots of soft kisses along my eyes, nose and ears on this day, not only from Maggie, who has also taken to kissing me on the lips, but from Kariba and Tortilla.

Yoshi, with the characteristic white scar on his left cheek, seems to have discovered me as well, grooming me voraciously all over the eyes and head, sticking his own head down through the opening of my shirt (buttons removed, courtesy of Tortilla or Sabrina), and coming to me for comfort when he is attacked by one of the more dominant males or females. Jagger—the scrawniest of the bunch—is also beginning to find me a source of comfort, particularly at the end of the day when time comes to take the babies in for the night; and Sabrina, not one of the mediums who previously seemed most drawn to me, quietly devours a carrot on my lap.

I'm fitting in, I slowly find . . . just becoming one of the family.

●　●　●

Before I know it, my stay at C.A.R.E. is drawing to a close. My last day of official work begins with three crises: Elena has been bitten by one of the suricates that morning when she went to feed them, and late last night, Kim got a call from her husband in California, who's been ill, suggesting she might have to go home. Rita's reaction to this revealed everything about how she views the human/baboon hierarchy. "Imagine," she commented when she related the news of Kim's husband, "having to choose between your husband and a sick baby!" The "sick baby" she was referring to, of course, was Diva!

Meanwhile, up in Star *Hok*, Paprika had been nearly choked to death when one of the other baboons stole the new volunteer Kora's T-shirt and got it wrapped around her neck, forcing Lee, Kim, and Zurika to jump in and rescue her.

Suddenly, I begin to feel a deep welling of emotion come over me. I am actually going to have to say *good-bye* to Dennis and Maggie, and to all the others.

. . .

On the day of my scheduled departure from South Africa, I rent a car and drive from Phalaborwa back to C.A.R.E. to say good-bye to Rita, Lee, Bennett, and my "children." No sooner have I arrived, but that I commit one of those "human errors" people so often make with baboons—namely, underestimating their resourcefulness and intelligence—and leave my car outside the volunteer lodge rather than locking it up behind one of the Center's fences. Though I've removed my backpack and all obvious signs of food, I should, after all this time of living day and night among the baboons, know better. By the time I've walked down the hill to Rita's house, members of the wild troop have had at the car in search of food, ripping the passenger side mirror right from it. And I, of course, have only myself to blame.

When I walk into Rita's living room, Suzi, who is there with Lee, is so glad to see me she leaps onto the sofa to play. What a change from those first days, when she ran and hid from me! But there's also been bad news during the night: Nelson from the "Nut Village" has died of pneumonia after eleven years at C.A.R.E. When they shaved his chest to do the x-ray, Rita tells me, they found that a number had been tattooed on him by the experimental lab that used him as a subject before his rescue by C.A.R.E. One can't help ponder the irony of it all: The dark resonance of Rita's German past rearing its head once more.

"Where will you bury him?" I ask Rita.

"Up the hill with all the others, behind the Nut Village," she replies.

"And do you put a marker up for each?"

"No," she smiles. "I remember where they all are. . . . And that's where I'm going to be buried too." Which was to take place, I never would have imagined at the time, much sooner than either of us ever suspected.

Part Two

"BECAUSE THEY NEEDED ME"

Prologue

In order to forestall my critics I would like to begin by saying—yes, this is an emotional book. It consists of experiences had and observations made during my long association with a wild baboon troop, our living together, our interactions, my own feelings and, I have no doubt, also the feelings and reactions of the baboons. All my life there have been protracted fights and arguments in the world about whether animals have feelings and "emotions," whether they feel pain, love, and hate as we do, and whether they should be allowed to have names. What ridiculous and convenient arguments human primates come up with to give themselves a scientific license to do to their fellow primates as they wish!

Looking at the historic record we have in respect of our dealings with each other—not so long ago bushmen were hunted and killed as "vermin," the African race—i.e. black skin—was declared inferior, and we are still struggling to overcome this classification, the total embarrassment the Great Apes present us with right now, in light of now available genetic facts.

This book was written out of my desire to share my experiences, impressions, and my love for a misunderstood primate species. If I have made mistakes, so be it. In my understanding, greater minds have done so in the past.

Rita Miljo
Philaborwa, South Africa
March, 2008

Chapter 1

A HITLER YOUTH
(1931–1945)

I was born February 18, 1931, just two years before Hitler came to power, in Heilsberg, the "land of dark seas and forests" in East Prussia, the most northeastern corner of Germany. The area where I was born has since been split up and is today divided between Russia and Poland. My family, middle-class Catholics, lived in a small village called Heinrichswalde, some ten kilometers from Tilsit on the Memel. At the time, this little river comprised the German border with Lithuania which, in turn, was part of Russia. The nearest town of any cultural and historical significance was Koenigsberg, capital of East Prussia, some one hundred kilometers away. It was always a huge event—seeming like a trip halfway around the world—when my mother took me to visit our family there.

As might be expected, my memories of home are of a wonderland of beauty, low fertile wetlands and large spreading dark forests stretching deep into Russia, with water everywhere. People lived on dairy production, there were lots of fat black-and-white cows, milk everywhere, and the Tilsiter cheese, produced by local farmers, was considered a delicacy.

I remember being sent by my mother to fetch "fresh" milk from a certain farmer who owned a brown-and-white cow. I duly insisted that my milk had to be from a very particular cow, named Musche. As usual I took a shortcut across Musche's owner's field. High up in the sky, a solitary airplane approached, something that was very unusual in those days. It brought a stark reality into my head: *So this must be war.*

I made very sure I got what I wanted by attentively watching the farmer milk Musche for me. All the water in the wetlands caused many narrow little waterways to form, as well as small dams that contained myriad of miracles in the form of water creatures of all sorts. I spent much of my free time lying flat on my stomach, inspecting and observing these creatures. To my mother's utter horror and despair, I often also brought quite a few of them home.

Summers were short and very hot, and every respectable farmhouse had a resident stork roosting on its roof, encouraged by old wagon wheels the farmer had mounted in order to entice them to come. Every spring, the day the storks returned to their nest called for a big celebration, and ensured the farmer's good luck for the year.

Winter Sunday walks turned into trips into fairyland. Winters were long, harsh, and incredibly cold—temperatures could easily reach minus 35 to 40 degrees Celsius. I had to wear handmade fur boots, and we ploughed through meters of snow, with only my nose sticking out over the top.

From a very early age, I was encouraged by my father to develop a deep love for animals. Sunday mornings, he took me on long walks into the forests, where I learned about wild boars—that they were dangerous and to be avoided—and all the various wild deer. My father kept me very busy. He showed me how the local forester, his friend, looked after the wild animals in all that cold and snow. Shelters were erected into which my father's friend placed hay for the deer, and I was taught how to make feeding places for local birds that didn't migrate to warmer regions. My father would also show me how not to get lost in the forest by marking my way along the trees. Did he know, I have often wondered, that he would not have much more time with me?

In the meantime, dark clouds were gathering in Europe. At a very young age, I discovered the Hitler Youth and volunteered to join them when I was only eight years old. (Normally every child was to be enrolled at the age of ten.) My father was a party member himself, but my mother remained tight-lipped and silent about the whole thing. At the age of nine, I became the youngest Hitler Youth leader in the entire Province.

I liked being a Nazi because it was all a competition thing, which I very much enjoyed, and because I was good at such things. I liked sports, liked being the best at all sorts of things, which was how Hitler captured children. I could do things I wasn't normally allowed to do as the only daughter of an overprotective mother. Only today, in hindsight, do I understand the total madness our families were subjected to.

The days the war started are indelibly imprinted in my memory. Hitler had made sure every good German could listen to his propaganda and invented the people's radio, the *Volksemfaenger*. Every household contained such an item. On the eve of the invasion of Poland, Hitler was making one of his speeches. As usual, I didn't understand much of what he said, because he spoke with an ugly Austrian accent. (Obviously, the Fuhrer could do no wrong and it was I who was to blame). My mother became more and more agitated, and was jumping in and out of bed (she was a very beautiful and temperamental woman), making comments like, "My God, he has done it, he is starting a war" or "No, no, so he is coming to his senses, there will be no war," until she finally collapsed in a heap, sobbing bitterly. The next morning she sternly directed me to go and see my grandmother and tell her that the War had started.

Still, life didn't change very much for my family during the War. My world was complete. My father had been called into the army months before the war even began, but, in the meantime, it had become apparent that the Fuhrer could never be wrong and the eventual outcome of the War seemed to have been decided way in advance.

My father returned home after the conquest of Poland. He had somehow become a stranger to me, very quiet and withdrawn, not at all interested in my animal stories any longer. With my usual inquisitiveness, I tried one night to find out more. My parents thought I was fast asleep, but I was hiding behind the open door leading into the living room. What I saw really disturbed me. My father was openly weeping, a thing no upright German man would even contemplate doing. I overheard him saying to my mother, "If there is a God in heaven, we cannot win this war after what we have done to the Jews in Warsaw."

"But the war is finished" I heard my mother reply.

"No, my dear," he said, "it is only beginning." My father was then a young man of twenty-nine, and war would comprise the greatest part of his life.

The war in East Prussia only began to affect us when Hitler declared war on Russia. The fun time in the Hitler Youth was now over: There were no more sports competitions; now we had to learn to march and behave like soldiers, which I found rather boring but was nonetheless still good at. Through school and the Hitler Youth combined, we had huge tasks to fulfill. We had to find, dry, and prepare medicinal herbs, vast quantities of which were weighed and controlled monthly; we had to collect old iron and paper and things to be "recycled," although that word was not yet in use. All this was part of our contribution to the war effort.

And then the real horror began to strike me personally. One morning, a burned-out vehicle drove into our garden. Out stumbled the driver, collapsing before he could reach our door. My mother rushed out and recognized her oldest brother, my uncle Kurt, who just made it to our house before he totally collapsed. His story was horrible: He had been ordered to take wounded soldiers from the front line back to a field hospital; there, he had been attacked, and his vehicle caught fire. The poor soldiers had cried out for mercy, but he couldn't stop to help, and ran for his life. They had all burned to death, and I saw for the first time the real horrors of war. It taught me to hate. The Fuhrer had taught our young minds to hate, kill, and survive. And we had taken his lessons seriously.

The end of the war, 1945, found me in West Germany—Bavaria to be precise—miraculously still united with my mother and father. But we had no idea where the rest of our family was. We knew we were unable to return to East Prussia, not that my father would have allowed it. In spite of the terrible post-War situation, he had decided to leave the comfortable countryside in Bavaria, and go to a city where he could find a job and a school for me. So the entire family trekked up north to our destination, Hamburg, a large and totally bombed-out city.

The strange thing about the human mind is that one forgets the bad things about the past and remembers only the good things. Gratefully so, and perhaps it is the safety mechanism the mind employs in order to keep one sane. It would not be until the Hungarian uprising of 1956 that I would have the one and only nervous breakdown of my life, and by then I was already living in South Africa.

How often am I asked about the War, with all its horrors and madness: "How did you find the War?" "Good," I would answer, "it has made me what I am. All my life it has helped me not to give up on man."

After long weeks of traveling at the War's end, begging for rides with all our belongings, we eventually reached Hamburg. It was a dead town, destruction and death everywhere. Entire suburbs were recognizable only by the shells of burned-out apartment buildings. As usual, my father knew what to do. With eyes trained by war, he soon identified some buildings he thought still had viable cellars that could be converted into living quarters. Once we had located such a place, it was only a question of salvaging the necessary building materials in order to render it somehow fit to live in. In my eyes, my father's greatest achievement was his retrieving a toilet basin that was dangling from a burned-out wall some two or thee stories up. It was perfectly suited for what we needed, and begged to be rescued. My father somehow accomplished it, accompanied by my mother's wailing and prayers.

Now this, our "cellar," was a gift from God. It consisted of four rooms, which even had some bunk beds in them Very soon our grandmother, our father's sister, Herta, and her three children joined us. But there was simply nothing to eat. A loaf of bread had to be shared among all of us (eight people) for one week. I really don't know how my poor mother even managed to keep us all alive, but she had talent and imagination. Many of the precious belongings she had rescued from East Prussia found their way into the hands of the surrounding greedy farmers in return for a bit of food. My father remained honorable; the best he could do was to pretend not to notice our inventiveness.

And then the Neumann family began to prosper once again. My mother and I joined a gang of "organizers" who waited for the coal trains to enter Hamburg. Approaching the bridges across the river Elbe, these trains had to slow down. This gave us youngsters the opportunity to jump onto the train and throw off the coal as fast as we could. I jumped on the train and my mother gathered up the coal. Two or three large buckets full of coal a day were enough to keep us warm, and we could exchange the rest for food. I could elaborate on the many ways we survived, but suffice it to say that my mother was very good at it, and we probably owed her our lives.

My father soon again got a government job (men were scarce in those days), and then there was the question of finding a school for me. This wasn't so easy, since most school buildings had been bombed out. However, some ten kilometers from where we lived, one of the most reputable girls' high schools, the *Kloster Schule*, opened up once more. Their building was damaged—no windows, no doors, some shaky walls. But nonetheless we had a building that eventually housed three schools, working in three shifts. Admission was through a selection process, which I succeeded in passing. It was one of the happiest days of my life when I could go back to school, whether it was starting out on foot to walk the ten kilometers at 4:30 in the morning—a lonely and spooky walk through endless dead streets lined by burned and bombed-out buildings—or going late at night for the last shift. The midday shift, of course, was the best.

This was the most profound soul- and mind-shaping period of my life. I can only say that I owe my whole being to the teachers I had. Imagine where I had come from—born into and raised in the Third Reich, all my values shaped by Hitler and Hitler alone. Our parents had to shut up, or were too scared to talk to their children. Then came the end of the War, the total collapse of everything I had believed in. Now, on returning to school, a new world opened up for me. I discovered that there was a Shakespeare, for instance, and every bit of knowledge and intellect Hitler had withheld from me as soon as it became known that its origin was Jewish now opened onto my horizon. It was simply overwhelming.

Our teachers were members of the elite class. We had several well-known professors who had been demoted because of their membership in Hitler's Nazi party. Each and every one was special to me, and I truly pity today's young people, who do not have the privilege I had. I could devote an entire chapter to each of them, thanking them and acknowledging how they have influenced my life. But the most outstanding among all of them was Frau Dr. Politz, the previous school principal, who had been expelled from her position because she was Jewish. She was the first to return to cold, hungry, war-torn Germany in 1945. She became my teacher supreme, my idol, my source of strength and wisdom. Mark well, all this coming from the youngest Hitler Youth leader in East Prussia!

I matriculated in 1949 and, of course, given my passion for animals, wanted to study veterinary medicine. It was perhaps a good thing this didn't materialize: In hindsight, I would have become a lousy vet. University entrance was very limited for female students at the time. Ex-soldiers received preference, and I only managed to be admitted as a psychology student. This soon bored me to tears and I quit, just in time to help my mother, who was dying of cervical cancer. The tragedy of her death was that I had a little brother, who had been born during our "coal-stealing" era; he was seventeen years younger than me, and only three years old at my mother's death.

It was a tragic time. My father finally gave up on life after my mother's death; he drank and drank and drank. I had to get away in order to survive, so I took a job in a factory involved with electrical ceramics. Since I had to work odd hours controlling the furnaces in which the ceramics were burned, a small flat came with the job. So I had a place for myself and my little brother to live, and the possibility of watching over him while working, as well as a reprieve from my father's excesses. I also had a huge task my mother left me with—that of finding a mother for my little brother Peter. It was a very hectic, responsible time, all of which left me with a stomach ulcer.

I did all that, however: finding the perfect mother for little Peter, persuading her to marry my father, and eventually having a life of my own once more. I quit my factory job and went in search of my passion—animals—once again. In Hamburg, the Hagenbeck Zoo was always looking for people. Strangely enough, working for the zoo in those days immediately branded you as someone asocial. Respectable people didn't work at zoos, and my family immediately intervened, my grandmother informing me they could no longer be seen with me in public if I took the job. I rebelled, and took it anyway.

Working at the Hagenbeck Zoo was a good time for me. The Zoo was progressive, it had begun developing "open enclosures" and the zoo administration was actually open to suggestions. My first task was to look after the New World Primates Section (how significant for my future life!). The weather in Hamburg wasn't good for primates: they were kept in "air-conditioned" houses, very prone to pneumonia, dying readily. I remember having difficulty with their eating, and trying to figure out what a tropical forest might look like. So I began decorating their plates with flowers, making them look more interesting and more "tropical." In other words, I was subconsciously applying my psychology background. It worked, and they ate much better.

I had a boyfriend—correction, a fiancé—named Lothar Simon, whom I am not sure I intended to marry. But I had a lot of respect for him and he was studying in Berlin, so we weren't always in each other's hair. But I don't think I was ever very good "marriage material" and was far too independent for the time.

Of course, you can never really explain the chemical reaction between people—it's either there or it's not there. But I remember, for example, how my own family break-up came about. At that time in Germany, you were expected to marry and date within your own class. And then I had these stupid little idiots "dating" me—borrowing their father's Mercedes to take me to a concert. Now what, I asked myself, had some guy who could borrow his father's Mercedes, and then inherit his father's surgical practice, and so on, ever achieved? Sure, he wasn't really interested in becoming a doctor, but that was a tradition, and my family nodded and said, "Yes, this is marvelous; this is the guy you're going to go out with."

But that simply wasn't for me. I picked a poor farm boy like Lothar instead, and I had to teach him table manners, and I to be very circumspect about things, so as not to offend him: *this* glass, no not *that* glass, for white wine, and so on. I mean—how can I say it?—he was himself. "If you want me to take that glass or that glass to make your grandmother happy, I'll do so, but don't inconvenience me,"—that was his attitude. And I must say I was intrigued, and terribly impressed, by him.

I was only nineteen, just out of school, when we met. But everything he had done, and everything he achieved, he had done by himself. He worked to be able to go to the university, because his parents were poor. He was brilliant enough to get help from the people he worked for in order to go to university, but he did it all himself. And he had a bloody little motorbike, and I appreciated that. But, when I started dating him, my family disowned me. And I said, "Well, that's okay. That's what I want."

Lothar also had twin sisters. That was *such* a joke. He was studying at the Technical University in Berlin, and I knew one of the twins—she worked at the same place I worked. Well, you could see she was his sister—I mean, she had his dark hair and dark eyes. But he was always talking about the *other* twin, who was in far-eastern Germany at the time, and I hadn't met her. And for some reason I just got on my little motorbike and drove to Hamburg from Berlin—you know, a surprise visit. And it was one of those apartment doors where you had to ring and say, okay, I'm so-and-so. And I got there, and as I got to the door there was somebody who had rung already and I slipped in and went upstairs, and there was my fiancé with this *gorgeous* blond sitting on his couch. And I said, 'Oh my God! I'm sorry—I'm interrupting you here!' And I went out the door and got back onto my motorbike and went back to Hamburg.

I thought to myself: Now I've caught him! And then he phoned me and he got on and said, "You know, you've really made a bloody fool out of yourself. That is my sister!" And I said, "Yeah, tell me another one." I had known the other twin—she was dark-haired with dark eyes. And here was this blond beauty with blue eyes—and they were twins? "Now tell me another one," I said. "I don't mind—if you want to, have her." And so he made this poor sister come to Hamburg to convince me that she was the other twin.

I never outlived that. For years afterward, he would tease me about it. It was such a surprise! I mean, you get there and you think you're giving him a lovely surprise, and there is this beautiful blond lying on the couch. And I said, "Shit, and I've been sitting on my motorbike for three hours!" I was annoyed—of course I was annoyed.

One day Lothar told me that he had to go to South Africa for a week or two to deliver and demonstrate a machine his professor had developed. My heart began pounding—Africa, the land of my dreams! I put it to him to look around and find out whether we shouldn't go and live in South Africa. In response, he sternly told me, "if you are good at what you are doing, you'll do well in your own country; you don't have to run to Africa." I didn't reply, but my thoughts went something like this: "What a pity, you might miss your chance with me, my friend."

As it turned out, he didn't miss his chance, and my dream came true.

Chapter 2

AFRICAN DREAMS
(1953–1963)

The KLM "Flying Dutchman," the most up-to-date passenger plane of its time, made a sweeping turn over a sea of lights, and the old lady beside me, who had taken me under her capable wings said, "There you are; that's Johannesburg." I was thunderstruck. Is *this* my Africa? The place looked as large, or larger, than Berlin! It was ten o'clock at night, Christmas Eve, 1953.

As the plane made a turn to land, I realized with a shock that I was actually arriving ten days later than scheduled (that's another story), and all I knew of my dear Lothar was his post office box number—no telephone number or street address. Would Lothar be there to meet the plane? I voiced my misgivings to my traveling companion; she was a dear old lady and probably recalled the madness of her own youth. "Don't worry," she said, "if he's not there, you can always come home with me."

Well he *was* there, and he was fuming mad: "Where the hell have you been? I've been running to each and every plane arriving from

Europe for the last ten days!" Now I was *convinced* that I wouldn't marry Lothar Simon. But only two months later I changed my mind. Africa in 1954 was not very female friendly—as a woman, I couldn't go anywhere without an "escort." White women were rare, and I received a marriage proposal at least once a week. So in February I suggested to Lothar that we get married after all. He merely smiled.

It was a good marriage at the time, but only because of his efforts, not mine. I was very, very independent, and became upset if he restricted me in any way, and he knew it. He either had to give me space or he didn't have a wife. And he was wise enough to do exactly that. We were good friends, had laughs about it all, even had laughs about the girls that chased him, because he was a very good-looking man. And I said to him, "Why aren't you a bit more selective? I mean, what do you see in her? Why, she already has false teeth!"

"How can I say no to a woman when she comes up and wants me?" he asked. So I said okay. It eventually turned out to be a very loose arrangement. I'm quite sure he didn't have his mind and his soul in it; that's why I was never jealous of him. I hated jealousy, because my father was very jealous—so much so that he made my mother's life into a misery. You're born with it, I think. You're either jealous or you're not. And I really didn't like jealousy. Because, really, what are we talking about basically but your own ego being wounded? The only thing that really bothered me was that sometimes he carried on a bit too obviously; and I said, "Why can't you be discrete about it?" But I never felt threatened by his choices. I never felt threatened at all.

In hindsight when I think back upon the men I have known in my life, I think I could have had a happy marriage with quite a few of them. I think the story of the great big love is just a little bit of a story. I mean, I never planned to marry my husband in the first place; it simply happened. When I came to South Africa I was determined *not* to marry him. But there were a lot of Germans here at the time, and the husbands needed wives, and, well, I thought I'd rather marry the devil I know than the devil I don't know.

Our actual wedding turned out to be a joke. I could have come into the country either on a marriage license or a work permit, and had said to Lothar, "Well, forget it. If you don't get me a work permit, I'm not coming. I've got to think about this marrying." So he got me a work permit, and I got here and I said, "I've been thinking about it, and I don't think I'm made to marry you." And, gosh, he really knew what I was like and he said, "Okay, that's fine—there's a job for you here. I'll see you." And that was very hard, because I spoke a kind of Shakespearean English, and an office job was very hard on me; it was, in fact, terrible. So after a few months I decided, okay, I'll marry him.

And I said to my boss, "I need the afternoon off." And Lothar asked me, "Well, what do you want to do? We could go to an office and have an office wedding, or we could go to a church." And I thought, well, an African church, that's not for me. So we went to this Justice of the Peace. My God, what a place it was! It was filthy and dirty, and we were given this piece of paper, this license, and I said, "You know what? I don't really think I want to get married here. There is a German Lutheran Church—let's have a look at that guy."

So we went to look at the guy, and he came from Southwest Africa, so he was more German than the Germans—an old, frizzled-up little man. And he looked very sternly at us and he said, "So, you want to get married?" And he turned to my husband and said, "Are you sure you are able to support a wife?" And my husband said, "Sure." And then the pastor said, "Show me your pay stub." So Lothar did. And then the Pastor said, "Oh my God! You're much too young to be earning so much money!" And then he turned to me. "And you?" And I said, "Well, I'm okay with it, if you're willing to marry us."

"Okay, you can come next Thursday," he said. And I asked my boss for the afternoon off again, and again he said okay. And then I said, "But we do need a cake." So we went to some German *Konditorei*. And we had a little Volkswagen Beetle, from which we had removed the front seat, because Lothar had been carting around engine parts.

I was sitting in the back seat with the cake beside me, and Lothar suddenly had to brake—and I sat on the cake! It nearly ruined my marriage.

So we decided not to have a cake; but then we decided we should have a flat, so we looked around for a flat, which we got. And I said, "You know, we should have a mattress. Let's forget about the bed. It's too hot here, but we should have a fridge." So we bought an old fridge for five pounds, and my husband being my husband, every damned thing he had to take apart to see how it worked. And then there was a huge explosion in the kitchen, and he had taken the fridge apart the night before the marriage. I don't know what happened, but it went *paaff!* So I said, "Now *you* speak to the pastor and postpone this marriage!" What a beginning! It was so funny.

Well, it was just he and I, and we of course had to find a guy who'd sign the pieces of paper, and I said to my boss for the third time, "I have to have the afternoon off." And he said, "Rita, why didn't you tell me you want to get married. We want to be there as well." So eventually it happened, and this bloody pastor was standing there, and it was just me and my husband and two or three people, and he gave us this huge speech about "Here are these two young people, all alone in the wide world, wanting to marry, and their families are far, far away," and oh my God! He went on and on and on, until he got me into tears. God, I thought, I just wish he would stop! And that was my wedding.

But here in South Africa, when I got married, it was also very difficult to be a woman on her own. In Germany, for example, there were lots of things you could do by yourself—you could go to the theatre or the movies or a concert on your own. But when I got to South Africa, you couldn't do that . . . you had to have an escort. You couldn't go *anywhere* or do *anything* alone, which was really terrible for me. If you were a woman alone, people thought you were for sale.

I remember, for example, that I wanted a nice flat. And I had to jump on the bus every morning to go to the office. And one day I was waiting for the bus, and some guy stopped his car and asked if he could give me a lift. I said sure, and, when I got to work, my boss's wife said, "My God, you're early!" And I said, "Yes, some guy stopped and gave me a lift." And she nearly had a heart attack, and said, "Don't you *ever* do that again! He could have taken you into the next hotel—because that's what you told him to do."

Yes, there were a lot of things I didn't know.

That all having been sorted out, where was I now going to find "my Africa?" I was bitterly unhappy. Johannesburg was just another ugly city. What I missed most were theatres, concerts, operas. Culturally speaking, there was absolutely nothing, but I was told "You have sunshine instead." I needed more than sunshine: Where were Africa's animals?

We had rented a small apartment in an upper-class suburb. When I opened my eyes in the morning, I calmly observed a group of large insects crawling on the walls and under my picture frames. Happily I said to myself, "This is Africa after all; at least there are insects." One day I took one of these insects to work to try and find out what it was. "Oh, those are bed bugs," I was told. A week later I remembered to look the name up in a German-English dictionary. My God, my mother would have had a heart attack! Bed bugs were the worst things you could ever come across! Why hadn't they bitten us, then? Not fond of European blood, I suppose.

Before we even bought a piece of furniture, we bought a second-hand Volkswagen Beetle. By now, our roles had reversed: Lothar desperately tried to make me like Africa. Every Friday afternoon we would leave the ugly city and find the real Africa. Quite logically, Kruger Park was usually our destination, and there I found what I was looking for. I also found so much ignorance. People told me the most unlikely stories and eventually I decided the best approach was just to be quiet and observe. This, however, took time, lots of time.

Again I was lucky to find someone else to teach me, yet another person with a passionate heart who was grateful that someone wanted to share his passion. His name was Dr. Kleynhans, and he was a very special elderly man who was also an ornithologist. He taught me everything I needed to know about South Africa: its history, the reasons why people hated each other, the Zulus against other black tribes, the English against the white Afrikaners, why I was frowned upon by them for speaking English (after all the Germans had lost a war against the English!). He was a very principled man and even sold his house as soon as his street's name was changed from Old Pretoria Road to Hendrik Verwoerd Drive. [Hendrik Verwoerd is a former Prime Minister who is considered to be the mastermind behind Apartheid in South Africa.]

Now, I found that I had something to teach *him*. In my short life I had come to know the folly of man. Many a town in Germany was renamed, first by Hitler in honor of his cronies, then by the Russians, then back again to the original names once the Russians retreated, and now the same scenario was taking place in apartheid South Africa (only to be continued by the present ANC government!).

We soon left politics alone, however, and I discovered another huge treasure Dr. Kleynhans didn't even realize he had. He had made thousands of bird recordings, as well as recordings of other wild animal sounds. Today this might sound simple, but in those days it meant spotting the bird, climbing into the trees with a primitive microphone, stepping back and waiting for the bird to reappear, and hopefully recording the songs or sounds it made. I spent a long, long time trying to catalogue these recordings for him, and I learned more than I would normally have learned in two lifetimes. I also accompanied Dr. Kleynhans on his trips into the bush and he was delighted to teach me. We traveled through what is now Zimbabwe and Zambia several times. Without the knowledge I gained then, I could never have undertaken my later travels. Sadly, Dr. Kleynhans soon died of cancer, very quickly and unexpectedly.

In the meantime my dear patient Lothar was busy making lots of money. This wasn't good for him, or for us, so I decided I would have to spend his money as fast as he made it in order to keep him sane and reasonable. I didn't succeed. It was not a happy time in my life, from which I learned one big lesson: that money definitely doesn't make a person happy. If one can buy everything one ever wants, one no longer wants anything at all. And there were "friends" forever hanging around Lothar, all of whom told him how great he was. He adored it.

And this is how I got us involved with little airplanes, which eventually caused the biggest tragedy in my life.

• • •

There I was, blessed with a too-rich husband who was quickly loosing his senses: Too much too fast and too young to handle it. In my own stupidity I thought the most expensive thing I could do was to learn to fly small planes. So I told Lothar that this was what I was going to do next. This time he didn't shake his head in disbelief; instead he pricked up his ears and said, "Let's do it together." At last I had found something he was also interested in.

So we joined a flying club, booked lessons and immediately became each other's biggest competitors. Once again I had thoughtlessly intruded on a male prerogative. A woman behind a car wheel was dangerous enough; a woman in an airplane was suicide for the instructor. I overcame this by being pretty enough to make these guys curious, and found an instructor brave enough to take me up in a little two-seater training plane. The routine was to obtain a private pilots license within forty flying hours, and the guys at the club immediately tried to get at this big-mouthed German, Lothar, by proving to him that his wife was actually the better pilot.

The first hurdle was which of the two of us would fly solo first. Naturally, our instructors pronounced me ready before Lothar was, but I had the wisdom to talk them out of it. When it came to navigation, my husband beat me hands down. I was forever getting myself lost, and Lothar magnanimously suggested we buy a little plane with lots and lots of fuel space. So our first plane was a Piper Cub with extra wing tanks, giving me something like seven hours of flying time. Not long after that, Lothar wanted something flashier and bought himself a Cessna aircraft. I decided I wanted to do aerobatics and bought a vintage Tiger Moth, the only plane at the time capable of doing aerobatics. Since I couldn't find an instructor brave enough to take on a woman in a Tiger Moth, I eventually got hold of an old Royal Air Force Manual and taught myself. Flying thus became the second great love in my life.

Flying as such didn't much help in my quest to explore Africa. The range of little airplanes wasn't far enough to make much difference, an added difficulty being that on the other end I would be stranded without transport. So it naturally happened that I mostly flew to Mozambique. There was this beautiful island directly across from us named L.M. (today called Maputo), and I was able to fly directly across the bay from there and land right on Inhaca Island. Lothar had bought and stationed a ski boat there permanently and I began exploring the nearby sea and coral reefs. It was really a magical time for me, with the freedom to do what I wanted. My husband didn't restrain me in the least, and money was no problem, except that there was too much of it. I did the most stupid and most wonderful things, and could have killed myself a dozen times in the plane and the boat by mere ignorance. But somehow I survived and, looking back, I realize that I was extremely blessed to experience all these things. This rich, superficial existence, however, also destroyed all of life's real values. I now had a marriage only on paper—divorce wasn't yet fashionable—and we lived our lives, met occasionally, had a drink and a laugh together, and then went our separate ways.

As is always the case, I got bored with having everything, and doing everything my way, and it was in one of my brighter moments that I bought a little piece of bushveld near Kruger Park. More and more frequently, I began to take refuge there instead of living it up and partying. Lothar flew in just once to find out what my latest fascination was. He looked around, shook his head, and said, "I suppose I should count myself lucky you didn't buy a place on the moon." He never returned.

Little did I know that this little bushveld farm would eventually become the center of my life, and the life of hundreds of baboons.

Chapter 3

THE FIGHT BEGINS

It was in the middle of the eighties when I made my final move from town life to my little farm in the Lowveld, bordering the Olifants River. I arrived with five wonderful Rhodesian ridgeback hounds; my beloved baboon, Bobby; and a very tiny caravan. In fact, the caravan was so small there simply was no room for five ridgebacks to sleep with me, and I constructed a comfortable "cave" for them underneath it.

During that first winter season I carefully wrapped the dogs every night in their blankets and had the shock of my life one morning when I removed the blankets and a *Mfezi* [Mozambique spitting cobra] reared its head. It had been lying there, very comfortable and warm, rolled up between the ridgebacks, and it objected to being so rudely awakened. I decided there and then that it was high time to build a proper house.

During my dark years following the loss of my family, I took a bricklaying course and, with the help of a very capable and talented

African builder, Long Piet, we built the house. It ended up being a little stone house; nothing was square, as I discovered when I wanted to put down floor tiles, but it was strategically placed between some old bushveld trees I refused to take down to make room for a square house. I tried hard to make as little impact as possible on my environment, and I preferred to live with all the wonderful creatures, rather than to destroy and "civilize" everything.

In the meantime word had apparently got around in the animal world that there was a small piece of wilderness where animals were welcome, where nobody shot at them or looked at them as the next piece of *biltong* [South African jerky]. And it was amazing to see how they made use of this refuge when shots went off all around us on weekends. Soon the wild baboons also arrived, endowed with the special intelligence all primates possess. I soon had a group of wild baboons huddling on our farm, then beginning to play and steal and make themselves at home as they realized they were welcome.

I watched them in amazement. What a marvelous opportunity I had to learn about them, study them, and thus be able to help my baboon orphans on their way to freedom. Although it was not always easy and required a definite way of life, I was determined to grab this opportunity with both hands. Looking at the anatomy of the mothers and then not knowing that it was a perfectly normal development after they had had their infants, I called them the Longtit Troop.

My passion for baboons would henceforth dominate my life and I think this passion was necessary, because living with baboons is not an easy thing to do.

• • •

Baboons have this uncanny ability to observe and almost guess your next thought and move. For instance, they only have to watch how things are being opened once in order to figure out how to do it themselves. To be one step ahead of them seems almost impossible. I installed "baboon-proof" burglar bars on my windows, but the doors were another problem. First we always tried to lock them. This was impractical, as the keys frequently got lost. I tried round doorknobs, but it took only a short while for the baboons to understand their workings.

Eventually a good friend came up with a marvelous idea: a simple clip inserted between the two holes forming the lock, so that we only had to turn the length of the clip sideways and we could open the door. To this day the Longtits haven't worked this out, and when I have ten to forty baboons in my house, only I am to blame for having carelessly forgotten my own rule about shutting the door properly, even if it is only for half a second.

Any thought of a garden, lawns, or flowers had to be immediately abandoned, but this really did not pose a problem. The beautiful wild bush completely compensated for the absence of flower beds.

. . .

It all began so innocently. The new Wildlife Rehabilitation Movement was just beginning to hit South Africa, with nature conservation neatly divided up between the "good guys" and "bad guys." One only had to avoid the bad guys and be nice to the good guys and all would be well. When I applied for a permit to operate a rehab center in our area, a good guy told me to contact Karen Trendler in Pretoria, who had just opened such a center. The only other one, called CROW, he told me, was in Durban. So I did just that, and Karen and I decided to join forces.

Karen was happily playing with swallows and other little birds, as well as hedgehogs and the odd buck. She was well liked by all of Nature Conservation—after all she had originally come from their ranks—and I was very happy to have her in Pretoria, seeing that I was so far away from everything. As far as Nature Conservation was concerned, we were seen as harmless little bunny huggers, not to be taken seriously. We had to submit copies of our intake registers every month, had our monthly inspection by one of the guys and, if an animal didn't get better within a given time, we simply had to euthanize it. I was told I could take in anything except for the five "vermin species."

And this is when our troubles began. Here in our area we still had a fairly healthy baboon and vervet monkey population. Those animals were slaughtered left, right, and center and the baby orphans needed help. Having my baboon Old Bobby around and having come to know what an enormously clever "person" she was, I simply could not turn my back on these condemned little souls. However, trying to help "vermin" was met with a very stern "no" from our government.

But, once again, fate intervened. I had an old friend on the other side of the Olifants River, a retired professor who was a very active Conservative Party member and a brilliant person to talk to. He also knew lots of people, and one evening while visiting, I mentioned my problems to him. He merely laughed at me. "My girl," he said, "why did you never mention this before?" It was 10.30 at night, but Professor Hoppies picked up the phone and spoke to his former pupil, Dr. Piet Mulder. "You can't give my friend Rita so much trouble. Come visit me next Saturday and bring along your permit book." And so it happened. Next Saturday arrived, as did the most important person in Nature Conservation at the time, and, as quickly as that, I had my permit. Being new to the game I didn't realize that a major miracle had taken place.

Apart from Bobby, I knew very little about baboons, and, apart from Eugene Marais' field observations, published in his book *My Friends, the Baboons*, not much had ever been written about them. It was my belief that in order to be of any use to the wildlife we wanted to save, we should know as much as possible about the ethology of the species we were working with. I thought a deciding factor for a wild animal to want to heal and get better would be if it were as comfortable and unstressed as possible. For a future return into the wild, it was also of vital importance that one knew exactly what this animal would need in order to cope with its newfound freedom.

My previous years of wandering in the African bush now paid huge dividends. I had asked a thousand questions, spoken to so many people, sat quietly and just watched for so long that I now realized I had quite a bit of knowledge that proved to be useful. The little baboons came rolling in and captured my heart and, before I knew it, I had only one passion: the baboons of Africa. From Bobby I had learned their language, their expressions of happiness and pain, what to do and not to do. Beyond that, I had to go back to nature and watch again. Nobody worried about me.

It was an established fact that baboons couldn't be returned to the wild, and that was it. I was astonished at how little had been written about them. I remember a story published by a well-known professor in the official magazine of the National Parks Board *Custos* about how he had returned his pet baboon, a female, to the wild by just dumping her in the Kalahari Gemsbok Park. When he couldn't find her a couple of weeks later, he proudly proclaimed his efforts a complete success. I had my doubts.

I knew from my observations that no functioning baboon troop would accept single adult females into their midst. One didn't need academic qualifications to understand why. So the simplest way of solving that problem seemed clear: *Why not make my own troops?* There were enough orphaned babies coming in; all I needed to know was the make-up of a normal baboon troop, the sex ratios, etc. We had to skip the age ratios, since the baby baboons coming in were more or less of a similar age. The fact that they were babies avoided the hassle of ranking—in the wild, babies inherit the rank and status of their mother, which females are stuck with for life—thus it was an ideal beginning. So, getting back to my artificial baby troops, they would happily play together as well as accept additional babies as long as there was yet no established rank order. I therefore had approximately 12–18 months to add to or change a troop. By the time they reached the age of 18–20 months, ranking had taken place and no more movement within this little troop could be undertaken.

I learned as I went along. There were the usual emotions one encounters in human children: Some little characters simply didn't get along, and some formed special friendships. Luckily, we had enough babies to try and form "happy" troops, i.e., to separate two fighting characters. It was most interesting to watch the little females form their alliances and sort out their rankings. I quickly came to the conclusion that they really were perfect little bitches who, whenever they saw the slightest advantage for themselves, used it shamelessly. Once the ranking was established, however, peace returned and all we now had to do was wait until the little creatures became responsible grown-up baboons.

For convenience sake, having in mind to monitor them as long as possible once they were released, I chose to limit the size of such a troop to, say, fifteen animals, twenty at most. Any more would have been difficult to keep an eye on. At a later stage, I moved two such troops next to each other so that they grew up being acquainted. This gave me the added advantage of releasing one group and then, if required, following it up with their neighbors, whom they already knew. It also facilitated my monitoring.

In the meantime I had the good fortune to discover Dr. Shirley Strum's writings, mostly her book *Almost Human,* which was invaluable to me. Here was a scientist who said exactly and loudly what I had to say about baboons. And coming from a scientist, her words were listened to, and this gave me a great deal of confidence. A lot of behavioral facts I thought I myself had discovered were cited by her, and I realized that I had re-invented the wheel on many occasions. But what did it matter? It at least proved I was on the right track. So our humble beginnings were happy and fruitful.

With the help of Bobby, I took these baby troops on long bush walks to observe how they would react to bush food. My theory was that if baboons were clever enough to find out that humans meant food and would invade plantations to get at the food, they should, conversely, be just as clever in recognizing bush food when they come across it. I was right, and I was confident that I didn't have to teach them exactly what and what not to eat once they were free. These bush walks were a special treat for them at the time, but really weren't at all necessary to their rehabilitation progress.

Today I realize that baboons instinctively know what to eat in the wild. This makes a lot of sense when one considers that they have learned to exist under vastly different circumstances and adapt to the foods available. As an example I can cite the Mosdene troop I released in 1996 on a game farm through which the Nyl River flowed and in which, consequently, there were many little dams and waterways full of fish. Within two years, my troop had learned how to catch *barbell* [catfish] in those dams without anybody ever showing them; there were no other baboons left to be able to teach them.

I also made a point of feeding my baboons bush food, such as *maroelas*, whenever they were ripe and plentiful. This was always greatly appreciated by them. The only advantage wild baboons have over released troops is that they know their territory so well from growing up with their troopmates, who know exactly where what food will be when. On my Letaba troop release, I found that the wild crossover male would march off to a specific *maroela* tree in the morning. He knew the exact location of the tree and he also knew that this tree carried the day's best and ripest fruit. He had learned this by growing up with his home troop, but it takes a release troop quite awhile to find their way around new territory and come to know such invaluable facts, just as it has taken me a long time to fully understand my baboons' needs.

Chapter 4

ALONE AGAINST THE WORLD

Dark clouds were gathering around our happy little bushveld place, without my even noticing. I had friends, one of them a young black conservator whom I admired for his tenacity, against all odds, in actually getting his Nature Conservation Diploma at the Technikon. I was amazed by his dedication and love of nature and his acceptance of the petty officialdom that made his life a misery because he, a black man, was actually better qualified than his white boss. His wisdom and patience in dealing with all this amazed me and, talking to him, I realized how terribly underprivileged black children were, not being allowed to go every place, and therefore not being able to learn anything about their own country and heritage.

Through my friend I met black teachers and they began bringing their classes to our Center. I came to realize that all this talk of black people not caring about animals or the beauty of nature originated in the fact that these poor children had never been exposed to such things, never taught how to appreciate nature, and it was a totally amazing experience for me to watch them take in all these things that had been missing from their lives. The best thing of all was to observe them with my baby baboons. They seemed to understand them and, within no time, we had happy groups of baboons and children playing together, admiring one another.

This reminded me of a story Eugene Marais told in his book, *The Soul of the Baboon*, about *piccaneens* [Marais's term] in a village who disappeared for long periods daily. When the worried members of their village eventually went in search of them, they found them playing with a bunch of wild baboon youngsters downstream. In true human fashion, the children got a hell of a thrashing and were forthwith forbidden to carry on such "fraternization."

It was a happy and rewarding time for me. But danger continued to lurk. My neighbor, a man who had just left Zambia, the place he called home but was not prepared to share with black people, was very bitter and didn't like the happy sounds of laughter coming out of little children's throats at our Center. Out of the blue, I was suddenly summoned to Pretoria and questioned about who had given me permission to teach those little *kaffirs*—the term they used. This had to stop, I was told, forthwith! The neighbors couldn't tolerate it!

Not even a week later, on my way back from a walk along the river with one of my baby troops, all hell broke loose. There stood my neighbor at the fence dividing our two properties with his gun blazing away at us. He was shooting to kill the baboons! The result of this ambush was that three of my baboons were left dead and a fourth quite badly wounded; and the laughing neighbor told me, "There will be more of it!"

And so World War III began. I was forever walking around with my shotgun, as soon as I heard that my neighbor was nearby. Many a time, when I caught sight of him, I simply aimed and fired—and I seriously meant to hit him. The only reason for me to be sitting here today and writing this is the fact that I was the world's worst shot.

But, by God, I tried! I think he knew it, too; however, he was unaware of my terrible handicap in not being able to shoot straight. And he resorted to other measures. One weekend he set out poison, and fifteen of the wild baboons wound up dying a terrible death on my property. Officially I couldn't stop him, either: It was his right to exterminate "vermin." My friends were seriously worried that I would eventually find a way of shooting straight.

A very special friend, a well-known reporter for the SABC [South African Broadcasting Company], suggested going public with our World War III story. She contacted my neighbor and invited him to participate in the program, but she was told he would prefer to instruct his lawyers to watch what she was up to with the program. This was a tactical mistake—you don't go attacking the media before anything has even happened. To make a long story short, after the airing of her story, it took exactly four weeks for my archenemy to put his place up for sale. Bad publicity wasn't good for business, and he was soon out of my hair for good.

This, however, was only the beginning of our troubles. I had made waves, unwanted political waves, and I ran into a wall of problems as soon as it was clear that I was going to continue to be trouble and wouldn't just quietly disappear and never be heard from again. This is when Karen Trendler decided we should part company, and there I stood, alone with my baboons against the world.

From then on it was open warfare, the government and its extermination laws against me. And I think I won many a battle. Once again, the political climate of the time helped. Being German, I also had many contacts to my former country and, when things got really bad, I threatened to expose the goings-on in the overseas press. This was not what the government wanted, so they never precisely applied the law to me and my baboons.

The time finally arrived for my first troop to be released. I was aiming to release them at about four to five years of age, when the females would have just come into estrus and the males were still too young to think seriously about baby-making; at that age, they were still manageable and accepted our leadership . . . up to a point.

The adventure of my life, our first release, could now begin. One stipulation of my permit for the rehabilitation of baboons was that I had to tell the authorities where I wanted to put my release troop. But when I approached them I was immediately told, "You cannot do this; it is against the law. It is not permitted to place vermin back into nature."

Long arguments followed. I reasoned that they had given me a permit to do this project, so I was entitled to complete it. Eventually I was told I *could* do it, but again I was reminded to let them know where I was going to release. I now had several options. With baboons having been eliminated wherever they clashed with humans, there were places baboons no longer existed. People had begun converting agricultural land to game farms, and the writing was on the wall that, in the near future, farmers wouldn't get all the privileges and help from the new ANC government. So I got offers to bring baboons back into places where they had lived before but had now been exterminated.

Two or three times in a row, as soon as I notified the authorities of my chosen release site, I was contacted by the property owner, who made very lame excuses as to why I couldn't come. I didn't understand all this, and became desperate. A very good friend of mine, who managed and lived at Letaba Ranch, a 30,000-hectare Government Nature Reserve adjoining Kruger Park, was Chief Conservator of Gazankulu at the time. When he saw my plight and despair, he offered to let me and my baboons come there.

I dutifully reported my new release site to the authorities. Two days later, my friend from Letaba Ranch phoned me. He told me that we now knew what was happening. "I just had a visit from some Nature Conservation official, who told me that they could not dictate to me, but that it would be advisable and in my better interests to not let Mrs. Miljo and her baboons into the reserve," he explained. When I phoned Dr. Mulder to confront him with his officers' tactics, I was assured he knew nothing about it and he was prepared to dismiss the officer who had visited Letaba Ranch.

This was precisely the breakthrough I needed. It also proved to be the most difficult release I had done. Letaba Ranch was teeming with the Big Five [lion, leopard, elephant, buffalo, and rhino] and also had a healthy wild baboon population. But we learned so much. For me, it was definitely the most exciting and memorable time of my life, beyond all my wanderings in Africa, far more, even, than my living through World War II and learning to fly and surviving a crash in a Tiger Moth.

One discovery I made, for instance, concerned the interplay between wild animals. I walked off with my release troop in the morning. The wild crossover male had quickly learned that he should communicate with me, which rendered his task of making the rest of the baboons follow him much easier. So he walked off, looking over his shoulder and making sure I followed, and my baboons in turn followed me. In time I doubled back and made up the rear, so that I had the whole scene before me and became a silent observer.

On these walks I noticed that none of the wildlife we met up with seemed to be worried about me. There might be a magnificent kudu gazing at us and I could pass within a meter; impalas carried on grazing unperturbed, as if I were thin air. I realized I was being accepted by them because of the fact that the baboons accepted me. They weren't making any warning cries, to which all antelope react immediately, so things seemed all right and there was no danger.

What a potential there would be for peaceful "baboon safaris," I secretly thought to myself, if only the baboons accepted others the way my troop did me! To this day I am very careful about making too frequent mention of this, as mankind has this dreadful gift of making money out of any situation.

* * *

Baboons in our part of the world are not very highly esteemed. In fact they are despised and persecuted. Somehow, their intelligence, inventiveness and gift of outwitting the "superior race" of mankind have always been too close for comfort, and enough reason for men to try and exterminate them. Traditionally, before settlers arrived in Southern Africa, baboons had a better deal. Local people, who were used to living with, and respecting, nature acknowledged their special cleverness. There are lots of legends, stories and folklore about baboons, and respectable local communities still call them "our people." But there are others who associate baboons with witchcraft and fear them. The very sad situation today is that the bad things European settlers brought with them, such as guns, killing, and large-scale destruction of the environment, have remained in spite of the official trend of today's government to emphasize and revert to traditional values.

Under the Apartheid government, laws were passed under which five entire species of South African wildlife are declared "vermin." These were:

The baboon
The vervet monkey
The bushpig
The jackal
The lynx or caracal.

It was reasoned that God was drunk when he made these species, having no regard for future European farmers and their livestock, and that this situation had to be rectified by a righteous government by ordering the total destruction of these animals. Strangely enough, these laws are still on the books today, and nobody seems disturbed about them.

My fight for these baboons' "right to live" in South Africa was, and still is, a long and difficult struggle. I have won many battles, have lost many as well, but the fact that I am sitting here in this beautiful part of the world with a troop of bright-eyed, happy baboons around me who are looking forward to an authentic wild baboon life—and all this with official permission and with a lot of help and encouragement from the public—shows me that I may just have won another battle.

Chapter 5

THE LONGTITS OF THE LOWVELD

The Longtit Troop has now been living with us for some fifteen years. Very few of its original members are still around. All the original males have been killed or have left, but the females who form the core of any troop have a few grand old ladies left. One of them is Eule [which means Owl in German], and I will begin with her story:

Eule and Vera were some of the first baboon fugitives to arrive at our farm. One simply couldn't overlook the pair—Eule's hair standing in all directions like a toilet brush gone mad, unkempt and fuzzy. She looked ancient, and that was some thirteen years ago! Her friend Vera only added to their poor image, if that was possible. She looked just as unkempt and disheveled. In addition, she was very emaciated and, on closer inspection, I noticed a tumor as big as a large potato on her left thigh. Watching them over the next few weeks, I could see that both belonged to the lowest-ranking females of the troop. Whereas Vera accepted her position with resignation, growing thinner and thinner (we had a drought that year and food was very scarce), Eule knew how to outsmart the troop without rebelling against her lowly status. She was fast as lightning when she saw the slightest advantage for her; she knew how to disappear within a fraction of a second and hardly ever got caught or punished by higher-ranking females. In short, she became *Eule*, a symbol of cleverness, cunning and intelligence. Vera was just her nondescript friend, long-suffering and plain, and in obvious pain.

Very soon Eule had figured out that I was interested in her. She would sit well-concealed somewhere, watching me. She quickly realized I meant her no harm, but her lifelong experiences with humans and her natural cautiousness in all situations prevailed, and she never took a chance of being caught at a disadvantage. Vera, on the other hand, was fatalistic. There I was, obviously friendly, and always having something good for her to eat. She depended on it and soon visibly filled out, looking sleeker and happier. However, her tumor kept growing at a steady pace. The time came when she found it difficult to keep up with the troop, lagging behind and eventually just staying near us when the rest of the baboons moved off.

More and more frequently I noticed Eule also lagging behind, and I don't think this was merely out of concern for her friend. She had very cleverly figured out that there were a lot of benefits and goodies to miss out on if she had walked with the troop instead. And in any event, her companions would be passing through again, at which time she could join them.

So it came about that I spent a lot of time with these two baboon ladies and I couldn't rid myself of the feeling that we communicated almost telepathically. Eule made it her business to know exactly what went on in my house. She was forever peering through the windows, knew what food was available and, by staring at me, almost willed me to hand her some bananas through the window. She created our "take-out" window, and it took no time at all before everyone in her troop gathered at this particular window hoping for handouts.

On such occasions Eule naturally had no chance to even approach or pick up anything at all. Many a time I caught her staring at me, and many a time I found myself putting some bananas in my pocket and casually strolling out to the clothesline behind the "Mamba" kitchen, only to be met by Eule, who was obviously waiting for me. It wasn't always the same meeting place, but meet we did, and I simply gave up trying to understand how we "arranged" these meetings.

And then came the day I last saw Vera alive. She was sitting near our little dam in the sunshine, waiting for me. I took some bananas and carrots and went to sit with her. I could see the suffering and pain in her eyes. The troop had left and Eule had gone with them. I offered Vera the food I had brought, but she refused to take any notice; not even the bananas could change her mind. Slowly she got up and walked towards the thick bush near the riverbank, looking back at me several times. I thought I should somehow end her pain, and it dawned on me that this was the last time I would see Vera alive. I tried to make sure to note where she was heading to hide, but she gave me the slip, like a little shadow. I only hope her end was quick and painless.

Eule returned with the troop but not once did I notice her looking for Vera. For her, only the present counted and life went on.

• • •

In all the time I have known the large female baboon we named Big Mamma I have only seen her produce daughters. Considering her size, I would say that none of her daughters developed their mother's strength and strong build. Big Mamma also seemed to "baby" her offspring longer than the other mothers did.

There was an occasion in our area when a great many snares were laid, snares of all sizes, from really strong ones—one of which incapacitated the then-alpha male, and eventually led to his death—down to very fine wired bird snares, set for trapping guinea fowl and francolin.

One morning, I was confronted by a horrifying scene. I heard a baboon baby's pitiful cry and stormed out to investigate—only to be confronted by Big Mamma. Of all the possible mothers it was *her* baby who was in trouble. My heart almost stopped beating. There was this little mite, maybe four to six weeks old, with one of those horrible bird snares around its neck! About five inches of the wire stuck out on one side, enough to annoy Big Mamma. She would pull at the wire to get rid of it, but in the process she was strangling the baby, until finally it went limp and unconscious. Then Big Mamma would let go. There was no way I could get the baby away from her, or get near enough to help.

Could I outsmart her? I armed myself with an old Teddy bear along with one of those bird snares that I had collected of the same make that now threatened the little baby and a mountain of bananas. Quietly I sat down near the mothers' meeting place, the bananas clearly in view. Mamma moved closer, her attention diverted from the snare to the bananas. Slowly and deliberately I put the snare around Teddy's neck, with Mamma watching me closely. Just as slowly and deliberately, I pulled the snare over Teddy's head and threw her a banana. This game went on a long time, until all the bananas had disappeared. Big Mamma's attention was now stretched to the limit, and she walked away. Later that day I went in search of her, expecting the worst, and eventually I found her. There she was, sitting contentedly near the dam, grooming her baby, who no longer had a snare around her neck! Coincidence? Pure luck? My imagination simply gone wild? Who cares—the baby was safe and sound and that was all that mattered.

Naturally, after all this drama, the baby deserved a name and we called her Riana, after a wonderful friend—Riaan—who loves the baboons as much as I do. Riana became a very special little baboon. She somehow developed such a trust and love for us, often walking with us, especially with Riaan, and waiting patiently for us to notice and, of course, spoil her.

Riana grew to approximately three years of age, and then tragedy struck again. Although I had repeatedly complained to ESCOM [Electriciy Supply Corporation of Malawi] about their unsafe transformer unit, nothing came of it at the time, and a freak accident took place in which two of the young Longtit baboons, one of them Riana, got terribly burned. Her ankles and wrists were frizzled away, cutting off any blood supply to her hands and feet. We rushed her to the vet, hoping to save her. But what kind of quality of life would a baboon without hands and feet have? With heavy hearts, we decided to have her euthanized.

• • •

Lucy was a slim, nondescript young female when I first noticed her, not very highly ranked, but also not right at the bottom of the ladder. She would probably never even have entered into my baboon stories, had it not been for her great illness. First, I noticed her becoming listless, trailing behind the troop and, one morning, found her lying near our dam, unable to move. The troop had moved on without her, so I could easily pick her up. Lucy knew me by then and, I think, trusted me not to hurt her—or maybe she was beyond all worry. During the day she grew rapidly stiffer until she became like a piece of wood. With her head drawn back and her teeth firmly clenched, she was showing typical signs of Tetanus. I wasn't too familiar with those signs at the time, but our veterinarian confirmed my suspicions, and we held out no hope for her.

I decided not to give up without a fight, however. Feeding her baby milk formula enriched with an occasional egg by means of a syringe, I managed to get the necessary sustenance into her. Thank God, she could still swallow. I tried to get her to relax with Valium injections and was greatly encouraged that, after two weeks, she was still alive and fighting. I realized that my main task was to keep her will to live going. She must have suffered tremendously, but I could detect a spark of life in her eyes. I further encouraged her by bringing her an orphan baby that held on to her and talked to her, and I cried when she replied in her own motherly way to the baby's needs.

And then, as it turned out, Lucy made it. After a long eight weeks her stiffness subsided slowly and she could eventually rejoin her troop. She soon forgot about her ordeal and, although I was always greeted by her enthusiastic lip-smacking, which is a way of greeting and saying "I love you" in baboon language, she remained a normal wild baboon. Not knowing much about the devastating tetanus disease at the time, I told my vet about my healing of Lucy. He smiled and told me not to be so cocksure. I may have worked a miracle with Lucy, he said, but such miracles didn't occur very often.

Unfortunately, he was right. Lucy later had another baby, which she mothered and protected. Some two years later, while looking after her next baby, I noticed a definite trend in her to encourage the baby to spend a great deal of time with her friend. Often I saw the baby being carried and mothered by the friend, rather than by Lucy. I found this "neglect" on Lucy's part hard to understand, but soon things became clearer. Lucy had lost weight, she was obviously not well, and I think she must have sensed it and was making provisions for the youngster to have another mother. This may sound rather anthropomorphic to some people, but knowing Lucy so well, having watched her being such a good mother, pulling her through the tetanus disease with the help of an orphaned baby, I had no other explanation for this strange behavior. Lucy soon vanished, her baby happily installed with her friend, not missing its mother and growing into a well-adjusted member of the troop.

• • •

Our Longtit Troop was, of course, wild and free to go wherever they wanted. They frequently left our property, especially during specific fruit seasons, such as when the marula trees bore their fruit. Looking them over when they re-appeared was always an anxious time for me. I would look for my special friends, such as Eule and her family. The males, of course, were always the first ones to be killed. Those were not happy days, and often I cried over my lost, murdered children.

On one of these reunions with my Longtit Troop, my eyes immediately fell on the plight of Mercybee. She was just another young female who had the ill fortune to encounter the wrath of man. A bullet had smashed her knee, which now stood out at a crazy angle, but Mercybee had made it home, intending to hang onto life. She survived, but her leg was permanently crippled, making it difficult for her to keep up with the troop. Very soon she developed her own routine, simply staying behind with us when the troop moved off, and waiting for their return. In spite of her handicap she managed to get herself pregnant and soon had a lovely little baby.

Her happiness only lasted a few days, however, when one of the dominant females snatched her baby from her. Poor Mercybee had no chance to retrieve her baby; she couldn't run fast enough, and the baby eventually died in the thief's arms. Mercybee was very, very upset, my heart went out to her, but there was nothing I could have done. And then she was pregnant once more. Should I leave her to her fate or should I help her? I wondered. I decided to help.

One day, when a now very pregnant Mercybee followed me into one of the enclosures to steal some food, I closed the door to keep her safe from thieving females. She didn't seem to object, made herself at home, and, with one of our small baby troops beside her, coped well with her new circumstances. Within a very short while, Mercybee produced another baby girl, and the baby troop next door made a huge fuss over the new arrival, Mercybee was spoiled and pampered and enjoyed her safe and privileged position. Eventually I decided to integrate her into the baby troop, and this worked very well. The baby is now part of a troop and will be released with them when they are old enough. Mercybee eventually rejoined her old troop. It was from this episode that I learned how to integrate grown-up females into a troop in order to give them a chance to freedom. It's a long hard road, but nothing is easy in this world of ours.

. . .

Poor old Tripsy did not come to my notice for a long time. She was just another female in the Longtit Troop. However, some six years ago, I spotted her when checking the troop on their return to our farm. Somehow they got themselves into trouble again, and there was Tripsy, totally brutalized and smashed to pieces, her left arm broken in two places, dragging herself along, bent over with pain that was obviously brought about by internal injuries. In spite of her severe injuries, she fled in a panic when she saw me.

What had men done to this poor animal? I searched for her for days and eventually found her hiding in thick bush. She could hardly move any longer, and therefore had to accept my coming close. The fact that she was even still alive totally amazed me. So I began to feed her—baby milk, bananas, and eggs. She accepted the food—she had no other choice if she wanted to stay alive—but her eyes told me how desperate and terrified she was. After a few days she could drag herself along and moved a bit farther on. I followed and gave her food. Her will to live was unbelievable. After some time, she began to move around again, but I had by now made it a habit to look for her in the morning. She never trusted me, or gave me the slightest encouragement or recognition; however, she gratefully accepted my food.

This went on for years. We had this standing arrangement of meeting in the morning, out of the troop's sight, behind the "mamba" kitchen. Tripsy would consume her milk, two eggs, and at least three bananas. By this time some of the troop's stragglers had discovered our little game and came charging back to drive Tripsy away. Most of the time we outsmarted them, and Tripsy slowly put on weight and looked better. She strictly stuck to our morning meeting times and I had to be there, knowing that she was waiting and that her well-being depended on me. However, there was no intimacy between us. Tripsy had forever decided that human beings couldn't be trusted and she tolerated my interference knowing that without my food she was lost. I was saddened by the fact that nobody in the troop took much notice of her, or tried to help or console her. On the contrary, it was I who had to protect her and make sure that she could eat the food I gave her.

Some time, during my younger years, when I was fortunate enough to travel the South African regions, exploring and learning, I had accompanied a German researcher who was trying to find what he called "wild bushmen" in Botswana. He was as passionate about his bushmen as I would later be about my baboons. He had studied and learned their language and told me the most amazing stories about them, their ways of life, the way they saw the world, and the way they lived and battled to survive in hostile surroundings. Bushmen lived and moved in family groups and he once told me that, if family members were too old and unable to move with them, they would make them comfortable with an ostrich egg full of water and some food and leave them behind. This was all done very respectfully and accepted by all, since the well-being of the clan had to come first.

I found this hard to understand at the time, having been brought up with Western ideas and emotions. Looking at Tripsy's circumstances, however, I seemed to understand better how the laws of nature worked and were applied by communities. Nonetheless, given my emotional upbringing, I just couldn't accept leaving her to her fate. And so Tripsy and I fell into a routine of saying good morning to each other every day as I gave her her daily bread and provided the means for her to stay alive.

In this way Tripsy lived for another five to six years, sometimes looking better than ever, and sometimes not. She was always the loner; as I watched the Longtits playing by the river's edge, I occasionally saw her walking past, but nobody took much notice of her. Eventually age caught up with her, and she looked progressively more

fragile and even seemed to have trouble breaking up the eggs I offered. I could have let nature taking its course, but when I thought
of the tremendous effort she had made, against all odds, I decided to
take the "human" approach.

We tranquillized her slightly and put her into a "granny cottage"
enclosure. Here she could look out over the river and most of the day
was right among her troop, who came and went right past her. The
first two days, when she tried to talk to them reassuringly, she was
mostly challenged and many of the females charged her cage, sending
her screaming into her sleeping quarters. It took her only two days
to accept the fact that she was actually safe and nobody could hurt
her. Then she sat in full view of her troop, contentedly munching her
bananas, still making friendly greeting grunts, looking dreamily over
the river. All she needed was someone to talk back to her or give her
a loving little groom. But then life is never perfect and I always expected one day to find her having left us, hopefully peacefully and not
lacking any physical comforts.

It was December 2007, two days before Christmas, when Tripsy
left us. We found her that morning, her back legs totally paralysed,
unable to move any longer, a possible organ collapse in her abdomen.
A dose of kethamine took her out of her misery and we euthanized
her. She went peacefully, not knowing she was going to die. Have I
done the right thing in prolonging her life by some seven years, life
she fought so desperately hard for? I will never know, one simply does
what our human brain tells us is right in our eyes. The only thing I
know is that I spared her suffering and agony in death. She was my
friend and there is another empty space in my life.

• • •

De Jager arrived at C.A.R.E. in November, 1997. Apparently he was
spotted in the middle of Polokwane [previously Pietersburg], and an
officer from the Department of Environmental Affairs had been sent

out to shoot him. Could it be?—a fully grown baboon male in the midst of the capital of Limpopo Province?

Fortune smiled on him in that the officer, a Mr. de Jager, genuinely cared for wild animals and so, instead of using a bullet, used a dart gun. This is how he arrived at C.A.R.E., and so he was, quite naturally, named after his savior—de Jager.

We were not sure what he was—wild baboon inadvertently straying into a town? Not very likely. Or an escaped "pet" baboon? He was very big, at least seven years old and in his prime. An escapee from a research laboratory? We will never know. He took up quarters in our Nut Village, where all our sanctuary baboons stay, so that we might possibly find out from his behavior what his past could have been. De Jager behaved impeccably. No fighting or swearing at neighbors, no breaking of things, a good appetite. We had nothing for which to fault him. Due to his good behavior we decided on an experiment. What if we freed him here at the Center and gave him the opportunity to integrate into the Longtit Troop?

But the Longtits were a difficult bunch, especially the old ladies. However, their alpha male at the time, Giovanni, was a kind and tolerant fellow. One morning, after breakfast, we opened de Jager's cage door—"Freedom, here I come." However, de Jager did not appreciate his long-lost freedom. It took almost three weeks before he even acknowledged the open door. In fact, we had to trick him by closing the door quickly once he ventured a few yards out. It took him another four weeks to move a few meters further away from the closed door. This behavior of his strongly indicated that he may have been a captive baboon before he came to us.

After that it got easier. Eventually de Jager ventured down toward my house, but had to battle with some of the young male contenders. Giovanni ignored him and de Jager made all the right moves, according to baboon etiquette. He sweet-talked the babies—what mother does not find *that* appealing? And soon some of the youngsters were greeting him enthusiastically when he appeared. Mothers moved closer and began grooming him; he seemed to have made his entire integration easy.

Then, one morning, all hell broke loose. Two boisterous young males teamed up to attack poor peaceful de Jager. He fought back bravely, but sustained a nasty hand injury. As quick as the fight had started, it was all over—with some of the sympathetic mothers helping de Jager! De Jager persevered and although not anywhere near the top of the male hierarchy, was quite content to be one of the ladies' favorites. His hand didn't look very good, but he managed.

. . .

A few months later tragedy struck the Longtit Troop again. Giovanni caught his arm in a snare and was soon taken by a leopard. The troop was in utter disarray. Every opportunist tried to take over Giovanni's alpha maleship. Four outsiders, huge fellows, appeared from nowhere and terrorized the troop. The poor females suffered badly, and de Jager was far too soft to stand his ground. Not a week after Giovanni's death, de Jager disappeared. Naturally, we all thought the leopard had also managed to overcome poor, inexperienced de Jager.

Months went by and eventually the new leadership of the Longtit Troop was sorted out. But we kept on wondering what could have happened to de Jager. All our searches failed to come up with the slightest clue. Amazingly enough, nine months later, there he was, sitting at our take-away window and, as usual, expecting some bananas. It was as if nothing had ever happened. The babies greeted him happily, the mammas lip-smacked a welcome and groomed him, and we were so pleased to see him again that he got away with mountains of bananas. Even his injured hand had healed so beautifully that he had almost full use of it again.

That year de Jager was the most desired consort in the troop. Almost every female made sure they would produce his progeny, all fabricated behind the alpha male's back, and de Jager was the busiest father one could imagine. But he had to pay dearly for his popularity.

De Jager made the fatal mistake of mating with Gretchen— Gretchen the bad mother—and fathered Little David. Little David was just six weeks old, pink-faced and big-eared, when Gretchen decided that motherhood was for the birds. David was dumped into de Jager's arms, and there he remained. Every so often Gretchen would dash in, feed her son, and take off again. It got so bad that little David screamed with fright whenever she appeared to feed him, and couldn't get back to de Jager fast enough.

All this placed some limitations on de Jager's love life within the Longtit Troop. I remember a very funny incident when de Jager was sitting in the sun, cuddling his baby. A young female, very much in need of a consort, gave de Jager the come-hither treatment, wiggling her beautiful rosette behind beneath his nose, trying to entice him into the bushes. But there was little David, clinging determinedly to his belly and claiming all the attention. De Jager desperately looked around for Gretchen, eventually found her, then ran up to her to dump David and go after his new ladylove. But he hadn't counted on David's devotion. Taking one look at his mother, screaming in disgust, little David charged after de Jager and, with one mighty leap, took up his rightful position on de Jager's belly. De Jager's reaction was rather comical. He obviously didn't have the heart to rebuke his now-contented little son, and so, seeming even a bit flattered, gave the new lady a sad look and settled down to babysitting instead of consorting.

But then, we also saw the side of de Jager we thought didn't exist. Tollgate, who was the ruling alpha upon de Jager's return, gave up his alpha position. He was an extremely handsome baboon and really hated fighting. He was, in fact, so clever in avoiding the usual male brawls that he had no battle marks on him at all. When the time came for him to step down, he did so gracefully. There was no necessity for him to walk away; he simply took over one of our "enclosures" as alpha male and pretended the Longtit Troop no longer existed. This way he had the better of both worlds—no competition and no fighting from other males, and the provision of good food which he could steal.

Now the Longtit Troop had a leadership crisis that could only be described as the "rule of the hooligans." All of the Troop's upcoming male offspring were getting out of hand. Three-year-old juveniles were challenging old mothers, four-year-old upstarts were trying to lay down the law, and the mothers and youngsters were having a very hard time of it. One morning I heard an infernal noise down by the river; everyone seemed to be screeching and fighting with everyone else. The youngsters were disappearing into all directions, peering at the goings-on from their hiding places. To my complete surprise, I beheld de Jager gone mad. He was screaming and foaming, shaking tree branches and storming after God and everyone, threatening to kill them. His main target seemed to be a mother with a small baby. She was just as thunderstruck by his behavior as I was, but turned around and tried to fight back.

For a moment, the "old" de Jager emerged. He stopped his attack on her, sat down and ignored her. Then he turned toward a huge sycamore fig tree, into which a large number of hooligans had fled and taken refuge. Shouting and screaming, he performed the most incredible acts of bravery, jumping for meters through the air, from branch to branch, scattering the now-frightened hooligans in all directions. All his precious babies and adoring ladies (including me) couldn't imagine what had changed such a soft old man into a raving lunatic. However, he had restored sanity among his troop and, for a short time, he was King Supreme.In December of 2003, however, tragedy struck. I hadn't realized how much I cared and worried about de Jager until the day we lost him.

He had been having a hard time; his teeth were rotting away fast, but the ladies were still fond of him and invited him to consort, much to the annoyance of the younger guard. His cloud of babies needed protection, but de Jager had a hard time keeping himself out of the firing lines. I noticed fresh battle scars on him, and, being aware of his wisdom and constant efforts to avoid fights and injuries, I realized he was not succeeding. Then one evening I spotted him, still surrounded by his family of youngsters, with a ghastly gash across his abdomen and a handful of intestines hanging out. We tried hard to immediately dart him so we could help but we couldn't hit him.

The next morning I rose with first light to continue my search for him. My faithful old Bennett must have had the same idea because we met at the river, looking for de Jager. Finally we found him, emerging from a clump of bushes near the river. He slowly walked toward me, moaning and panting, a large portion of his intestines hanging from his belly. What a terrible night he must have had, and still survived. Bennett aimed the dart gun and, when the dart struck him, he cried out loud, looking accusingly at me, as if to say, "Why do you hurt me also? I need help and not further pain." We raced to the veterinarian but it was too late. Part of his intestines had been torn beyond repair. All we could do for this charming old warrior was to allow him to cross over to his ancestors, gently and painlessly.

· · ·

As I mentioned previously, Giovanni was the alpha male during the time de Jager first made his entrance into the Longtit Troop. He was also a fine example of an ideal alpha male baboon. The troop lived well under his rule because he was wise and just and did not fly into temper tantrums in a hurry.

It is a fact that baboon troops very much depend on their leader's personality for their happiness and sense of well-being. If the alpha male is bad-tempered and easily offended, he will dish out punishment at the slightest provocation. His target baboon naturally won't fight back, but will pass his anger and frustration on to the next baboon, lower ranked than he is, and, in this fashion, one small fight will ripple through the entire troop until it reaches the lowest-ranked animal. A bad-tempered leader will therefore forever find himself surrounded by upset and fighting baboons. By the time his first reprimand has been passed down through the troop, he will have started another fight, and the next ripple will go through the whole troop, and so on. The permanent members of the troop, the mothers and babies, will just have to live through the reign of such a tyrant, but luckily it will not last forever.

Giovanni headed the troop for almost four years, and it was a time of bliss and peace. Poaching has always been a problem in Africa and it will be as long as people are poor and hungry. The area where our little farm is located was eventually declared a nature reserve, which prohibited any form of hunting. The snaring of animals also carries heavy fines. It took awhile until all landowners agreed to the change in land status, and one of the reluctant owners took advantage of the fact that the wildlife had become more trusting since the shooting had stopped. He owned a slaughterhouse somewhere and thus encouraged the indigenous people to set snares and sell him the carcasses for the butchery. It took some time to figure out where this enormous increase in snares had its origin, but we finally got to the bottom of it. However, many wild animals had to pay with their lives for this one individual's greed.

Giovanni was one of them. One late morning when the Longtit Troop arrived, I found him sitting at my kitchen door, staring at me and holding his arm out toward me. There it was, a snare made of thick fencing wire around his left arm! He obviously had managed to break the wire and, observing at the thickness of it, I marveled at the strength needed to break it, but he had done so. I was all alone that day; even Bennett had gone to do his monthly shopping. I realized I would have to dart Giovanni to remove the snare, but how would I possibly be able to follow him before he went down? It took a good two or three minutes for the drug to take effect, and, at my age, any baboon could easily outrun me.

Again I resorted to one of my old tricks. I went out to Giovanni, talked to him as if he were my child, all the while slowly walking toward our enclosed feed-room area. I was hoping that I could lure him into the enclosure, and then dart him once inside. That way he at least couldn't take off and disappear once I had darted him. Once again, I had reason to be utterly amazed at the almost human understanding baboons have. While walking, I was constantly talking to him, gently and calmly, and Giovanni followed me, hopping along on three legs. Once I opened the gate, it was a piece of cake: He calmly walked in and helped himself to food that was standing around. I carried on talking to him, telling him he shouldn't panic about being locked up, that I would now have to leave him for a minute to get help. Then I slipped out and ran for the dart gun. When I returned he was still sitting there peacefully, eating his sweet potatoes. The distance between the feed room area and my house was at least 300 meters, and it would have been extremely unlikely for any wild baboon to follow me such a distance under normal circumstances. And now I had to dart him!

I must explain that any normal baboon runs as soon as someone points an object at him, whether a gun or a camera or a stick. One can very often observe that baboons always try and keep a tree trunk, a rock, some tall grass or bushes between them and the person observing them—just in case. And here I had to stand in front of a grown-up, injured baboon male, aim the dart gun at him, and shoot. How would he react? I was pretty desperate, but had to do something. So again I started talking softly to him, explaining exactly what I now had to do. I actually think I was talking more to myself, in order to regain my confidence. Giovanni sat quietly, looking at me and chewing his food. I aimed the dart gun very carefully at him—I couldn't afford to miss and knew I was the world's worst shot. There was still no reaction from Giovanni—no protest, no aggression, nor any attempt to hide.

The dart went off and found its target perfectly. Giovanni hardly noticed being hit, carried on munching, and then slowly rolled over, mercifully asleep. I was elated, not knowing that my nightmare was only beginning. When I tried to remove the snare, I found that the wire had cut very deeply into his arm. Nothing on earth could move it! I tried and tried, crying, almost praying, to have the strength to help him, but it was in vain. I had to top off the tranquilizer to keep him under sedation, then rushed off to phone for help.

Luckily I managed to contact our local ranger, who arrived very soon. However he also had to struggle for quite some time before eventually managing to cut and remove the snare. Giovanni slept through the whole ordeal, and, when it started getting dark, I covered him with a blanket, deciding to let him rest and only give him his freedom the next morning. When I checked on him the next day, he was sitting quietly. He had helped himself to some food and was now watching me. Still there was no aggression or protest at being locked in. I opened the gate wide, which he acknowledged, but he took his time in eventually hobbling out.

We examined the arm and were sure it wasn't fractured. However, he would not be able to use it until he met his fate. Being so disabled, he made sure the troop didn't see him. In fact, he hid close to the feed room area and every time he saw me coming, he came closer, asking for food. This I gladly gave him, hoping he would recover the use of his arm in time. However, one morning there was no longer any Giovanni waiting for me. After a very thorough search of our area we eventually found him—or what was left of him.

Judging from all the signs, he must have put up a desperate fight. The grass was flattened around a big tree, blood was everywhere and only his head and limbs were left. Perhaps, due to his aching arm, Giovanni had gotten careless in failing to climb his sleeping tree thoughtfully and high enough, and so became an easy target for a hunting leopard. He must have fought back bravely, but, in the end, the odds were against him. He died like most of his kind, battling the odds of survival, hugely increased by human greed and selfishness. What is left for me is the memory of a truly worthy leader and his amazing understanding of his handicap, of my genuine attempt to help, and of his total cooperation. I am still wondering how we communicated. Did he understand some of my constant talking or did we communicate in baboon manner, as I did with Eule, almost telepathically?

• • •

Pumela—not a baboon, but a dog—is the most beautiful and obedient Rhodesian Ridgeback lady there is. She came to us as a puppy and grew up at the Center as part of the team. She learned at an early age that everything we called "Baby" had to be watched and pampered by her; she also learned that killing anything was altogether out of the question. At an early age she made friends with the Longtits and the Longtits learned that she was not to be feared. It was amazing to see how these wild baboons knew that Pumela was no threat to them. Even the mothers trusted her and, whenever people came and observed this harmony, we could point out that baboons do not actually tear every dog apart, but only defend themselves when attacked. And most dogs have been taught by humans to kill baboons on sight.

Unfortunately, however, the Olifants River is teaming with crocodiles and we had to watch carefully so that Pumela didn't fall prey to them. For this reason she only had controlled freedom and we knew where she was every moment of the day. One day, however, we weren't really watching, and she had disappeared. This was a strange thing in itself, as she had never shown the slightest desire to go exploring. We searched everywhere, but she had vanished. With a heavy heart, I prepared myself to never find her again.

Late in the afternoon, the Longtit Troop came into the Center as usual, trying to steal food and then retire to their sleeping trees. In the midst of the troop, there was Pumela—tired, wet and muddy, but very happy to have had an outing with her friends. We were later told that she had been sighted with the baboons some three kilometers from our Center, playing and being very much an honorary member of the Longtit Troop.

● ● ●

Billie came to our Bobby as Buta, meaning something like "little brother" in the Afrikaans language. He was one of three poor souls that the Mpumalanga N.C. authorities confiscated from some kind man who had initially saved a little female baboon, raised her, and made her the love of his life, naming her Jenny. Little Buta and Vleermuis, two small boys, joined Jenny later—that is, until the authorities stepped in and decreed that this was not allowed under the laws of the country. All three were shunted off to a so-called rehabilitation center, which at the time was run by a highly emotional and unstable ex-barmaid.

We heard about the unhappy trio and began negotiations to bring them to our Center. It took us almost six months to convince our ever-efficient officials that it is not a mortal sin for three orphaned baboons to cross a provincial border in order to give them some hope for a normal baboon life. We eventually succeeded. For Jenny it was unfortunately too late to be accepted into one of our existing troops. For Vleermuis and Buta, whom we now called Billie, it was easier. Being little boys, they readily settled into a group of youngsters destined for release into the wild when grown up. This should have been a happy ending. But it was not for Billie.

One morning, while inspecting our enclosures, we found him unable to walk. In fact, he seemed to be totally paralyzed from the waist down. Our initial diagnosis was that he might have fallen overnight and broken his back. X-rays taken by the local vet, however, revealed nothing of the kind. The vet for IFAW was called in and was equally baffled, but very methodically began ruling out this, that, and the other. Billie had the good fortune that one of the biggest and best private hospitals in Johannesburg agreed to give him a Cat scan to get to the bottom of his problem. So he was packed up carefully and taken to Johannesburg, accompanied by our chief animal keeper Bennett, whom he loved dearly, and our devoted vet.

The outcome, however, was bad. It was found that Billie had a soft tissue growth in his spinal column that eventually paralyzed his legs. There was no hope and Billie was to be euthanized the next day. And there I was, sitting at my computer and trying to come to terms with the situation. Billie had a short, but hopefully happy, life. He had more attention and medical care than many humans and, best of all, we could end his misery and let him die now, without having him suffer any further. And yet he was a little person, in my care, and it was I who made decisions concerning his life or death. And I knew that death would be tomorrow. I think the worst thing about death is knowing of it in advance.

Good-bye little chap, who knows how soon I will join you.

. . .

One of the worst scenarios that can befall our Center, and the vervet monkey world as well, is a kind of gastroenteritis. It seems to hit very suddenly, and especially attacks young animals. By the time the signs appear, it is usually too late; almost overnight the little animal becomes lethargic, very thin, and listless. The treatment we have usually tried is immediate doses of Flagyl, reinforced in severe cases by another antibiotic. In our most recent case we used a Purbac emulsion, Ematrol, to stop the vomiting and running tummy. And then one can only sit and pray, administering small dosages of glucose water so that the baboons do not vomit it out again; and, in very severe cases, we administer drips.

Today I am sitting here, feeling very, very sad. On Monday we took a little girl out of Spinnekop's troop—she was about eight weeks old and displayed all the telltale signs. But she put up a brave fight. I had never seen such severe symptoms. By Wednesday, she was vomiting blood, and it was simply a battle against the fluid coming out at both ends and trying to keep little bits and pieces down. It's Saturday morning now, and the little one has just breathed her last breath. She was so courageous, devoting her last bit of strength to calling out loud, holding onto me—and then it was over. She really wanted to live, and I wonder whether there was anything else I could have done or tried. When one sees the hardened attitudes of our doctors today, refusing treatment when there is no money to pay for it, one wonders where the soul-searching of these gentlemen is when they lose a patient. I am so sad and devastated that I failed here.

. . .

Freddy was no gentle giant like Digit [one of Dian Fossey's favorite apes]. But what Digit meant to Dian Fossey, Freddy most certainly meant to me. There comes a time in the lives of all of us who have worked so closely with wild animals that our souls are touched and our lives changed forever. Freddy was just a very lovable baboon youngster, and, though I am far from being in the league of that legendary lady who has done so much for the understanding of our great apes, he was that special life-changer for me.

Freddy has been gone for nearly eight months, and it's only now that I can speak of him and of our wonderful closeness. It was a profound trust and friendship that were offered by him, a totally wild animal who took the first step in showing me his love.

When the time comes in a little baboon's life that its mother thinks it should be on its own and she begins thinking of having another baby, life can get pretty tough for the little chap. If the baboon troop is of the size it should be, there's a good chance that one of the old males, already past his prime, will gather his own offspring, those bewildered young baboon lads, together. Sometimes you can see one of the old guys walking along with a crowd of some ten to twelve youngsters around him, watching and copying him, eating what he shows them to eat and whatever falls out of his mouth and, of course, being protected by him. The first time I saw Freddy, he was part of such a group of youngsters, the old man being Scarface, a very old and wise baboon indeed. He knew what life was all about, and he taught his mentees very well.

Every morning they would appear at my kitchen door, asking whether there was anything to be had; naturally, there always was. But then a disaster occurred. One morning, there was the usual crowd of youngsters, complaining, crying and very upset, at my kitchen door looking for their morning handouts—but no Scarface.

I never saw him again. I took pity on the forlorn little group, who very soon dispersed to go their own way and follow their own destinies. But there was Freddy, persistently staying around me, wanting to be noticed and talked to. And, of course, he became quite spoiled.

One day, sitting by the river, something jumped on my back, two hairy little arms encircled my neck, and there was Freddy, tentatively trying to suck on my ear. I was thunderstruck. Never in my wildest dreams had I expected a totally wild animal to take this first step and break the sacred barrier of DO NOT TOUCH of his own free will. I had lived with and known his troop for more than ten years, but he was the first to break this barrier. And it has remained like this ever since. Since that initial time, I have had many of the young baboons come to touch me, explore and search my pockets, and treat me as one of their kind. However, Freddy was the first to do so.

It was a time of utter happiness and closeness. Wherever I went, Freddy would quickly be by my side, walking with me. He loved to come storming from behind and jump onto my back and I was allowed to carry him piggyback for hours. This was touching when he was little, but quite a heavy burden when he became bigger. Of course he benefited greatly from his special friendship with me. His status in the troop grew: Nobody dared touch him. When he behaved badly and really should have been punished by one of his superior troop mates, he would take refuge on my back. And, of course, he made sure everyone was aware of his special status.

Freddy had a passion for cameras, and I think that in his short life he became the most photographed baboon ever. He was masterful at posing and creating situations in which he would be positively admired. I will never forget the time we were visited by two members of the local police force who were looking for some robbery suspect. Freddy came storming in, jumped on my back, and made sure to look as if he meant business. The two law-enforcers quickly took refuge in their car, preparing to flee, and Inspector Mathebula said, "We can see, *you* don't need any protection here." What a farce it all was, and Freddy and I had a good giggle.

And then came the day when Freddy no longer came for his morning bananas. We searched everywhere, but the days dragged on and there was no sign of Freddy. The logical explanation could only be that a crocodile had taken him. Unfortunately, little Freddy may not have realized that not everybody regarded his status as untouchable, especially not crocodiles.

My life will never be the same again. Although Freddy could be so naughty and pompous, and oh so human, he really changed my life. He also changed my entire relationship with the Longtit Troop, as I previously mentioned. Within a few days, another little fellow tried to step into Freddy's shoes—we called him "Little Fred"—and all the other little guys treated me like their long-lost grandmother. All of a sudden, there was no more "no-touching" rule. This can get pretty hairy when you're confronted with a big fellow who weighs some thirty kilograms. But Freddy was the first, and was special, and I will never forget him.

• • •

Tarzan was beautiful, with a sleek, muscular body, not the usual dark color but a shining light grey, and when he walked he displayed all the arrogance and self-assurance a healthy young male baboon on the lookout for another home can possess. That is how he arrived here at C.A.R.E.

There comes a time in the life of every male baboon when he has to abandon his home troop. He may have been the alpha male, with all the might and power of an African dictator, yet nature's laws will eventually catch up with him. He will have reached the point when he will run the risk of mating with his own daughters, or outsiders will have moved into his troop trying to force him out, and nature's law dictates he must give way and go. He must find another troop and new companions to accept him, where he can begin afresh, becoming their new leader and fathering his children. He will provide new blood for the new troop, from which another resident leader will have to go.

Tarzan knew the rules, they were embedded in his instinctive memory, but he was still young, arrogant, and impatient. He did not understand that the baboons at C.A.R.E. were all man-made orphans, being brought up in small troops to be released back into the wild when old enough. All he saw were beautiful, desirable young baboon ladies, who in turn were totally taken in by this new good-looking baboon Adonis. So Tarzan caused considerable havoc among the residents at C.A.R.E. without really furthering his mission in life—to move on into another troop, take over, and introduce new blood.

With heavy hearts we decided he had to be trapped and moved to another locality, where he could do what nature expected him to do. Trapping him was easy—he was so arrogant and self-confident that he stepped right into the trap cage to get the bananas and eggs, which were his due anyway. He didn't immediately realize his mistake, but tried to be nonchalant about the whole matter and keep his superior image going. We intended to move him some twenty kilometers upriver, where he would find other wild troops he could approach. Since C.A.R.E. is situated in a newly established nature reserve, we saw no problem in making the move and approached the local chief ranger, Tom Yule, for permission to move him. "No, we don't want him" was the reply we got.

The Balule Natue Reserve consists of a few thousand hectares, extending along both sides of the Olifants River, which eventually flows into the KNP [Kruger National Park]. Knowing the policy of the KNP, who have been eliminating their baboon population over the years to such an extent that one hardly sees them there any more, we had no intention of putting Tarzan at risk by crossing into that region. But here we were, dealing with a private nature reserve recently created by so-called nature lovers, who now ruled that there was no room for a beautiful male baboon in his prime.

Let us examine these new private nature reserves. Part of Balule was created weeks before the end of the Apartheid area by absentee landowners who feared that their land would be taken away by a new government. The move worked well: Not only did they keep their land, but the price of property shot up sky high—it was the "in" thing to have a game reserve in the lowveld.

So Balule is still growing. A lot of people made a lot of money buying plots from poor whites and selling them as prime property in a "nature reserve." The running of these private reserves is left to committees, who have not the slightest idea how to go about it. There is, however, one thing they think they know: Baboons do not fetch the right price tag and at this stage are not "glamour animals." Their time will come. One only has to see what happened to the most maligned animals of all—the wild dog. It finally got its celebrity status, even if it is too late now. When we approached the almost defunct Department of Environment of Limpopo Province, we were told there was no place for Tarzan in any of their defunct provincial reserves. The self-declared "Eden of South Africa—Limpopo Province" had spoken.

Poor Tarzan. Take a good look at him: The planet has been shrunk to nothing for him. Will humankind, in particular our community of "nature lovers," ever have to pay for the way they treat their fellow creatures? Yes, eventually each and everyone will leave this earth just as naked as they came into it. No medals, money or power can be taken along. But then poor old Tarzan did not understand that his life was cut short because he was not glamorous enough or pricey enough, not suitable for a trophy killing that brings in big money. He was just a beautiful healthy animal who begged to be able to live for another ten years, and our nature lovers and the "protectors of fauna and flora" (i.e., highly paid government officials) denied him this small request. So he had to die in order to be free again.

Local worker David Malatji, food provider and driver.

Longtit mother and baby in the sun.

Denis, M.B.'s best friend among the mediums.

Rita, May 2007.

A happy longtit after a successful raid on the food truck.

M.B. on his last day at C.A.R.E., with an infant who got the worst of a fight.

Young infant clinging to back of longtit mom.

Denis grooming M.B., Icarus facing camera.

Rita and her assistant, Lee Dekker, May, 2007.

Rita consoling a newly-injured infant, May, 2007.

Longtit family, gazing out toward the Limpopo River.

Denis and his sister, Maggie, in serious contemplation with M.B.

Longtits; closest male is Bushbuck and farthest is Foot.

Chapter 6

THE GOD OF LOVE—A CHRONICLE

So God and I had an argument and decided we really didn't need each other. This wonderful benevolent Christian god of love— either a creation of peoples' need to blame somebody or thank somebody for the goings-on of this world, or else a cold-blooded brilliant monster who created our world and then turned his back on it, no longer interested.

I spent the night trying to keep a little baby alive and I lost. And I feel terrible. He was only two weeks old, two weeks of hell with an immature mother who didn't know what to do with him. Eventually we rescued the little chap after he had been tossed around by her like a rag doll. We should have done this earlier, but, like good little clones of the "conservation" community, we were reluctant to separate a child from its mother. So this little mite was born to hang on and desperately fight for the bit of love and caring he never got. Every part of his little body was bruised and hurt. He didn't dare even utter a sound, for fear he might get another beating. Thankfully he accepted the milk bottle and with eyes tightly shut tried to get some nourishment into him. All through a day and a night, I kept vigil beside him, anxious to keep him alive and give him the love he so desperately needed. He tried, tried so hard to survive, but his little tortured body didn't make it.

I feel bad, guilty and useless. Why didn't I see this coming earlier? Why did I stick to all these great human rules about not interfering with a mother and child relationship until the child is dead? Why does a so-called mother have the right to torture her own child? Why on earth does anybody dare to talk about an all-loving god who cares about every sparrow that falls out of a tree? I think our human race is totally crazy, having invented all these idiotic concepts. And last but not least, I question why I am so upset. Is it my own need to care for this little thing and make good what went wrong? Is it my own needs I am so upset about, or is it the total waste of life and the helplessness of this abused creature?

I have buried him and I must admit I haven't felt so bad in years. Is all I am doing just for nothing, there are millions and millions of such sad senseless tortures and deaths all over the world every day, so why do we even have the capacity to feel so bad about it?

As I am sitting and writing this, I am being called out to look at the most amazing thing I have seen in years. Down by the river beneath a huge fig tree, a young bushbuck is being groomed by a young baboon, who is thoroughly inspecting the tick colony under his tail and cleaning it. The bushbuck stands still and enjoys the treatment. Thousands of further questions cross my mind, but I better not get into that now.

April, 2005. I've had a bad day. The baboon babies have just settled into their sleeping quarters with bottles and blankets, and I am sneaking out to have a few moments on my own by the river. It's playtime for the Longtits, before it will grow dark in ten or fifteen minutes. Everyone is going full blast: The youngsters are wrestling, cartwheeling, fighting, and teasing the old girls. But the old girls don't mind. Their bellies are full, they've had a good day, and even Gretchen invites the odd youngster to take a ride on her back. Scruffy comes and looks at me intently, then carefully begins touching and grooming me. Little David bounces around, sees us and comes storming up to displace Scruffy. Tripsy slinks by, looks at me, and gives me a quick lip-smack. And here comes Little Freddy, now quite a "big" Freddy, and puts his arms around me.

I'm in the process of discouraging such intimacies. Soon Freddy will be a huge male, one who should not take such liberties. Thinking about whether I should tell him to go, my heart nearly stops. About three meters away, a young elephant bull lumbers past; he could smack me with his trunk if he wanted to. I decide to remain stone still and am grateful for little Freddy's arms around me. Maybe the elephant mistakes me for a baboon. The baboons don't seem worried about the elephant; they hardly give way, and he walks on. It's always amazing to see how silently elephants can move; one minute they're there, the next they're gone. Freddy, having done his "protective" bit, walks off to find a decent sleeping branch.

What a magical moment! Who will believe me when I try to tell this story?

May, 2005. A happy, lovely day. Darryl, one of my earliest volunteers, had joined us again on a full-time basis and taken a load of waste to the local rubbish dump. He came back and reported to me that he met with the resident Rubbish Dump Troop and saw a youngster struggling to follow the troop, with terrible injuries to his head and body. Although the chances of finding him again were very slim, we immediately jumped into the car with our darting equipment to help the little fellow. When we arrived at the spot where Darryl had last seen him, I understood that we needed a miracle to be successful, but we tried nevertheless.

After searching for a good two hours, the miracle happened: We found him. Crying for help from among his troop, he was hiding under a clump of grass where we could easily pick him up. His skull had a very nasty fracture and his right leg seemed to be broken. Yet he had managed to drag himself for a good two hours behind his troop in order to survive. I couldn't understand why his mother wasn't there to carry and care for him—most likely she had been killed.

We were so happy to have found him and to be able to help him. We immediately took him to our veterinarian, who treated the head wound and stabilized him with a drip to combat his dehydration. He then gratefully ate every morsel of food we gave him. Since our vet had no X-ray equipment, we had to revert to a vet who could do the necessary X-rays and there we established that the break was very high up on his thigh, near the pelvis, and required a pin.

I had already tranquilized the little chap so that we could handle him. However the vet insisted on using gas for the operation. He claimed this was the latest and most advanced equipment, and this made me smile. More than sixty years ago, during the Second World War, I had to have a piece of bomb shrapnel removed from my arm, and the field hospital doctor had apologized to me for using gas. There was nothing else available. When I mentioned this to the vet, he only glared at me. A sawed-off shampoo bottle had to be held over the little guy's nose, and I was to operate the button to determine how much gas he should get. To be fair, the setting of the pin was done very neatly and professional. I breathed a sigh of relief, but then the vet decided to have another look at the head wound. The gas was previously dispensed on below half strength, and I was now ordered to turn it up to full force 5. I questioned this, but was again met with an icy stare. "Do as you are told."

Five minutes later, when I gathered Braveheart (as we immediately named him) into my arms to take him home, he was barely alive, breathing very shallowly. Another ten minutes later, during which the vet really sweated to revive him, and he was gone.

I was devastated. His bright eyes are constantly before me, trying so hard to survive and having so much hope, with a full stomach, a warm and comfortable night behind him, and, for a wild little animal, so trusting that we would help him. All our efforts had been for nothing. Braveheart had to die to satisfy a professional's vanity. What are we humans actually made of? Might it be total evil? Can we truly say that we are made the image of God!

Year's end, 2006. A bad, bad day. I spent half the night before, checking on Hobbit Foot, telling myself that if, we could get her through the night, we might yet win. But it was not to be so. We pulled her through the night—only to lose her a couple of hours later. So I had to conduct a double burial, Hobbit Foot and Blind Boy. Then I remembered that my stepmother's ashes were still in the cupboard. My god, they had sent them to me a year ago from Germany! So . . . another funeral.

And then I spent some time by the river. It had been raining and the river at last was full of water. There were lots of floating tree stumps, etc., and on and on went the water. If we were just another evolved species—and I believe we are—why on earth did we evolve this stupid sense of wanting to know whether there is more to us than just the "selfish gene?" Why have we perfected the art of founding one religion after another, and why do thousands of people claim that they are saved? And why don't we realize that 99.9 percent of all this is bull dust and we should not go down that road? By the same token, why do I say 99.9 percent? I wonder how animals think about all this. We certainly don't know. As I sat, waiting for Blind Boy and Hobbit Foot's grave to be dug, with both of them having their arms around each other and rolled into a snugly blanket with only their toes sticking out, most of the Longtit members came past to look, sat down awhile, and contemplated the scene. Did they know what was going on? Did it affect them? Or was my "evolved" mind simply playing tricks on me.

I wriggled my toes in the river water, again trying to get some "supernatural" response from a croc, and got a real shock when a hippo came up for air about a meter from my toes. We humans are a pathetic species. Yet another thought crossed my mind: The religionists want us to believe we are created in the image of god. This surely is intended by them to make us feel good. But, for me at least, the human image is about the last thing one could term godly. And what if they are right and we *do* reflect God's image? Then this what God really is: lazy, vindictive, selfish, and vicious—and so I could go on describing the human race. It would make perfect sense, and would also spell doom for our planet. But then again, even an idiot can see that the planet is doomed.

And so, this is my good-bye to the year 2006. I just realized that my mother would have turned 100 in 2007! I wonder whether I will make it to the end of 2007. It doesn't really matter. Perhaps for Scruffy, since I don't believe anyone will spoil her when I am gone.

Early Easter Sunday, 2007. The first light creeps promisingly over the rim of the surrounding hills and our baboons make their way off their sleeping tree to greet me on the ground. They talk softly to each other until B.A., the second-ranking male, gives a loud call, greeting the new day. Then the whole chorus of voices rises, all of them talking loudly and excitedly. The moon, almost full, is still high in the sky.

We are in one of the most beautiful spots in South Africa, an area world-renowned for the huge meteor—supposed to have been the largest ever—that hit the earth some 2000 million years ago. Today it is a beautiful, peaceful valley, surrounded by steep hills and cliffs with the most interesting vegetation. Most trees produce berries and fruit, quiet clear springs flow from cracks in the mountains: a paradise for wildlife, birds, and, especially, baboons. However, apart from the happy chatter of our baboons and the occasional whistling of a bird, it's a silent world, a world in which man has created his own order and imposed his own rules. For the sake of a few maize fields beyond the hills, every bit of wildlife has systematically been exterminated over the last few human generations. The other day I heard the voice of a lonely jackal, soon silenced by the gun of a farmer who claimed the jackal had killed a newborn calf.

And yet there is hope. Many of the people here seem to become aware of the plight of our planet, and a concerted effort is being made to save the Dome Bergland and restore it to its former beauty. Thus it came about that we are here. A troop of our hand-reared baboon orphans, ready to be taken back into the wild, have had the good fortune of being offered this little piece of baboon paradise for their new home.

The sun has now fully risen over the hills and sends its first warming rays into the valley. I am sitting under a *Blinkblaar Wag'n Bietjie*, a wonderful food tree for our baboons, enjoying the warmth of the sun after a cool night. Most of the baboons are back in their sleeping tree, soaking up the sun and dozing in its warm rays. Einstein, our decidedly most clever female, devotedly grooms Peter Pan, the alpha male, and B.A., second in command, sits a bit farther off, obviously jealous, but pretending not to be aware of the grooming session going on between the other two.

A moment of magic, peace and well being for all of us.

June, 2007. Nathan must have been the oldest of the research baboons that we took on—must have been eleven years ago! From the beginning, he had always been a special boy. He had such distinct features, a very pronounced chin, and was very dignified and calm. Considering that vivisection labs only work with fully grown baboons and his lifetime at the labs, according to them, had been thirteen years, he must have been 7+13+11, or approximately thirty-one years old—even older than my very first baboon, Bobby. Along with Rhona, Sybil, and Gwinnie, his three ladies, he occupied the middle part of our Nut Village. But his special love had always been Saba, who died recently. I couldn't let Saba join the group, since the three old witches already with him were hell-bent on having a real fight with her.

So Nathan spent hours leaning against the fence that separated the two, and Saba devotedly groomed him for hours on end. Even at night I saw them huddling together through the fence, sleeping on the ground. But then Nathan was a bright boy and had worked out the fact that his enclosure was safe from any predators. The best feature of his home was a viewing platform with a thatched roof, very high up, from where he could look across the Olifants River and far into the lowveld. He loved spending time there, but lately I had noticed that he took some time climbing the long ladder to get to his favorite spot.

Being a very old lady myself, I decided to try that ladder, just to see how difficult it was. I also would have liked to enjoy the view. So one day, when nobody was around to watch me, I started up the ladder. Well, I got one helluva a good fright because not even halfway up I decided it was high time to head back to the ground—my time of climbing trees or other similar adventures was definitely over! My respect for Nathan grew—the old boy just didn't give up! I decided that it had to be the daily two eggs, spiked with multivitamins and Moducare, that we had given him for some years now, that kept him so fit.

In the meantime, I was convinced that Nathan couldn't possibly have had any teeth left, at least that's what it looked like, and for a long time now we had cut the food for the oldies into very small pieces and made sure that they got as much soft food as possible. The resident vervet troop, of course, was delighted. Being so small, they always found a way into Nathan's kingdom and raided the food whenever they could.

When Bennett came rushing in one morning to tell me that Nathan was foaming badly from the mouth and couldn't breathe properly, my first thought was that he might have choked on a small piece of food. What I saw made me think differently, and that it was serious. I was reluctant to dart him because of his breathing problem and immediately phoned the vet for assistance. Lizanne, our devoted baboon vet, was there within an hour. We darted Nathan, but found no obstruction whatsoever. But I was right—he only had four teeth left, and there were a few small pieces of apple and carrots in his pouches. He was examined thoroughly and the verdict was very severe pneumonia.

Well, many old humans die from that illness as well. We made him comfortable in the sickbay and I cried, having to put him back into one of those hated lab cages that stole thirteen good years of his life from him. Nathan must have felt the same, and felt betrayed. When I tried to hand him small pieces of bananas after he woke up, he severely scratched my arm and turned his back on me. In spite of all the medication, he didn't get better, and, after two days and constant nerve-wracking moaning from him, I knew he must have been in terrible pain and decided to take him back to the vet.

Lizanne also thought he should have responded to the antibiotics by then, and we both feared there was more than just the pneumonia to worry about. It's a terrible decision to have to make, about the life or death of any creature. But when I saw his suffering and thought what I would have wanted in his position, I knew the answer. It was simply unfair to subject him to so much pain, to possibly have to have him spend a long time in that hated lab cage. He was such an old man, and his special friend was now gone as well. So we decided to let him go to her.

The autopsy revealed that we had been right. Not only did he have this massive pneumonia and bad old scars on his lungs, but his abdomen looked terrible as well. I am not an expert, but it looked to me as if he had the most violent infection spreading through his entire abdomen, something I would imagine the worst appendicitis could resemble. And this had caused the terrible pain he displayed. Nor could this ever have healed again.

For me personally, the saddest moment was seeing him lying in the metal cradle on his back as Lizanne started to shave his breast. She paused, almost shocked, and looked straight at me. Right across his chest there appeared a tattooed number: 756. Yes, he had been in Baboon-Auschwitz, and after all these years here it was, staring right at me again: 756.

October, 2007. It was supposed to be a short visit to our Macnab release site and the Tito Troop. I wanted to take back a youngster who had decided to go it alone. There was nobody else at Macnab he could be with, and we decided to bring him home and take him out again with the second troop. We left shortly after lunch. Sue went with me, and I also took my little Rosie, as I didn't want her to be alone just as she was starting to bond with me.

Sue had Rosie in her arms in a blanket while sitting beside me. We pulled in at the release site to find the whole bunch of baboons sitting under the tree, seemingly bored. I told Sue we would leave Rosie in her basket in the car, and she opened the door to get out. It all happened so fast: Sue had hardly set foot out of her door when Tito jumped down onto the car roof, grabbed Rosie, and ran. I think he had mistaken her for a food parcel.

One of the old females ripped Rosie from him, having discovered that he held a baby. She ran off, and all the old females ran with her. I screamed at Stephen to follow them—what a terrible thing to be old and not mobile enough! Everything went far too slowly for me. As I went after them, most of the troop came running back past me and I noticed that it was all the youngsters and Tito. I grabbed a stick and tried to prevent them from running back toward Stephen and Sue, who were trying to get the baby back. I hoped to cover their backs, since I knew the troop would attack them.

This worked for a moment or two, as the bunch of youngsters were undecided, as was Tito. All of a sudden, however, a young female broke through the line and dug her teeth into my leg. This determined the onset of their attack, and some of them jumped at me, and I fell and was bitten from all sides. I thought that this would be my end, since there was no way I could stop them. I saw Tito, this big baboon, bent over me and looking at me. He didn't move but I realized that it was he who had bitten the wrist of my right hand, and now he was there, just looking at me. I wasn't scared of him, but simply sad. I realized it would be the end for all of them if they killed me. Stupid brainless animals, who didn't realize I only wanted to help and were only reacting to their instincts!

Forgive them, they do not know what they are doing: I heard those words so clearly that all of a sudden I realized how very easy it was to become a Jesus. Idiot primates, human or not human, all reacting in the same stupid manner. Tito turned around and walked away, and the entire mob followed him. I was bleeding badly, but could get up; and then Stephen returned with a badly mauled and dead Rosie. This was Paul's doing—he who was supposed to protect all the troop youngsters. What could possibly have motivated him?

I guess I was lucky that Tito's top canines were more than worn, so the bite on my wrist was painful and deep, but not dangerous. And would eventually heal. But poor little Rosie. I would have to analyze the baboon side of the matter later. Right now I simply had to struggle to straighten my mind out. How very easy it is to die—one really doesn't feel frightened, just a sense of waste and despair at all the stupidity and senselessness of this world.

The thought occurred to me that I might be kidding myself, and that perhaps this whole thing of rescuing baboons and giving back what was taken from them didn't really work. But how would I ever be able to return to a cup of tea and knitting, with no further aim in this world? Hardly!

December, 2007. The year is rapidly drawing to a close. A few days ago I went to fetch Tito home, and here is the story:

Over the last few months we carried out the second release of Groovy Troop at the MacNab Reserve. All went well, and we had good rains. Both troops are looking extremely healthy and fat due to all the wonderful food that is growing after the rainy season, which this year is thankfully normal, as it should be. The first babies have been born and we very appropriately named the first baby little Freedom—born to Groovy Troop. Groovy Troop, the second troop released by us at MacNab this year, are now also to be left alone. They have learned extremely well and the astounding part is that the two troops haven't even yet met. This proves that we must be doing the right thing. Both troops are still utilizing the sleeping trees we selected for them at the outset; there is so much food that they don't even find it necessary to spread out far enough to meet, and we have consequently decided—with the landowner's express blessings—to bring a third troop into his mountain kingdom in the new year.

In two months time Tito's troop will have been free again for a year. In April we lost young Paul; we found his body and came to the conclusion that he most likely died of snakebite, probably from a highly venomous black mamba. This, of course, left Tito with a heavy responsibility, and no backup in the troop. He had already been severely traumatized when, during their first release in the Vredefort Dome area, he had been replaced by Brian. Later Brian was shot and Tito had to take over once again.

When we took him out again on the MacNab release, he was actually already an old gentleman. At that time, we had decided to let him go with his troop and have another year or two of freedom, since there was also Paul to back him up. However, Paul died before Tito, leaving the heavy responsibility on Tito's shoulders again.

Two weeks ago, Stephen phoned me from the release site to say that Tito had walked away from the troop. He had gone to search for him, found him, then darted and caged him, since he thought Tito was sick. Why else would he have walked away from the troop? The situation now required some serious thinking and insight into "baboon psychology." Normally an old baboon will lose his alpha position if a younger and smarter baboon male pushes him out.

There was no such challenge to Tito. And yet he had left on his own accord. I immediately went out to the release site to have a look.

Physically, I found nothing wrong with him. Psychologically, however, he was not the Tito I had known: He was no longer arrogant and the "big boy in town," but greeted me with a sunny, and at the same time subservient, smile, and a big lip-smack. The last time I had met up with him, he was quite prepared to push me down the mountain had I not respected him. So, I took him home to C.A.R.E., put him into his old enclosure, and decided to observe him.

The guys next to him greeted him enthusiastically, groomed him, and Tito was obviously glad to see his old home again. He ate very well, took part in all the squabbles around him, ignored the present wild alpha male who had been claiming that section of C.A.R.E. as his troop. When I gave him his special treat for the evening—an egg, some bananas and dried fruit—he thoughtfully moved everything to just far enough from the fence so that the wild male who tried to glare at him from outside wasn't able to reach his goodies. Tito contentedly and gleefully chomped his food just an inch out of reach, apparently delighted in pretending to ignore the annoyed big fellow. He so clearly knew he was totally safe, and seemed to enjoy it.

Who are the people that claim to know better, I ask myself, and who would recommend that old Tito shouldn't have the right to what he wants and should be euthanized? *He* was the one to make the choice, and I think we must respect this. It is very interesting that Einstein had made the same choice before him, and had returned to us after *four* years of freedom.

Christmas Day, 2007. I feel as if I have fallen into an endless dark hole, for this has been the second worst day in my life. Late yesterday afternoon we received a phone call from our release site at MacNab. Dawie, who has replaced Stephen while he went back home to Scotland for a visit, told us that he had found two dead baboons near Groovy Troop's sleeping tree. He thought that there might be bullet holes in the bodies. Stephen and I immediately jumped into the car and, two hours later, arrived at MacNab. It was only a few minutes before dark. I drove like a lunatic to reach Groovy Troop's tree, but it was too late to see anything properly. We picked up the corpse of the youngest baby, Dale, which told us that her mother must also be dead—otherwise she would have picked up the baby herself, dead or alive.

Back at MacNab Lodge, all of us—the owner, Dawie, visiting friends—were completely stunned. The weirdest theories now came to light. For twenty-odd years I have been fighting prejudice in this country, first of all against baboons, but also against bushmen, *kaffirs* [a contemptuous term for Black Africans], and other so-called "vermin." So, the theories and explanations being put forward were nothing new to me and only served to sadden me even further.

This morning, Christmas day, we performed the autopsies on the two boys, Jake and Blade. They had been the deputies of the alpha male, Tobias. As a result, we are quite sure that this is what happened: With all the abundant and wonderful food, the troop had often returned early to its sleeping tree. The last time I visited, I met them early in the morning at the same spot. The adults were full of food and dozing or just daydreaming, the two little girls, Freedom and Dale, were puttering around, discovering the world. It seemed to me at the time that Freedom was more alert than little Dale.

The poachers probably burst in on the unsuspecting baboons, and their dogs probably grabbed little Dale. He was, after all, meat, and meat in any form is food. Dale's mother very likely stormed in to save her child and got attacked by the dogs. It was Jake and Blade's duty to go in and help. There must have been a horrific fight, during which Tobias, the alpha male, was able to lead the rest of the troop to safety. The autopsy had just confirmed the above when Dawie phoned to tell us he had found enough foot spoors and bloody trails—probably from badly injured dogs—to confirm our findings.

The question is: Where to go from here? Both Stephen and I are too devastated at the moment to see the light at the end of the tunnel, if there is one. All I could think of was to speak to one of the local

Chiefs. Stephen had his cell phone number, a cell phone being *the* status symbol for any indigenous South African. I told him that I was the Chief Sangoma of all baboons, that they had offended me, and I would now have to put a death curse on them. He said, "Come, let us talk before the cursing." So that's where I plan to go as soon as this happy Christmas season is over. They may decide to kill me before I can "curse" them, or they might genuinely want to talk.

This is Africa. Hopefully a further chapter is yet to be written by me.

Part Three

RITA MILJO AND
MICHAEL BLUMENTHAL:
A CONVERSATION ON BABOONS
(AND HUMANS)

Note: But there would, alas, be no further chapter to be written by Rita. Only this interview, which, among others, I taped over several glasses of white wine and some Beethoven, whom she loved, playing in the background in the very room where, five years later, she would meet her death. I simply wanted to know more about this brave and unusual person, and about the attitudes and convictions and—I suppose it is correct to say—the ideology that had shaped her unusual life. I wanted to know what she felt with regard to politics, love, sex, apartheid, her native country of Germany and her adopted South Africa, and how her years of working with baboons might have affected those beliefs. Sensing that she both liked and trusted me, and knowing her to be the kind of person who didn't easily reveal herself to others, I didn't want to let the opportunity of knowing her further, and more deeply, pass me by.

That Rita was a truly unique human being should be readily apparent from what has already preceded this. Part of her unusualness, I believe, had to do with her utter willingness to say what she felt and to treat human beings as individuals, for better or worse, without regard to matters such as race, religion, or any other "group" characteristics. I saw evidence of this in the respect and affection in which she was held by most of the Black South Africans who worked for her. At times, Rita felt—and said—things that were rather repugnant to me personally, and several such statements are included here. But what I always respected, and continue to value even after her death, was her willingness to be entirely present with her beliefs, and to value far more highly what people did than what they said. And not ever to be afraid to let them know.

Michael: Let me begin this way: If you had to say what the thing you have learned most from baboons is, what would it be?

Rita: I learned how people tick. I learned why people behave the way they do.

M: But you told me the other day that, after having spent some time with a friend who worked with chimpanzees, you realized that you could never work with those particular primates, because they were *just like* humans.

R: Exactly. Because they are deceitful, whereas baboons haven't learned that yet. So you learn from baboons the truth about yourself, what you really do. Chimpanzees have already learned to find the beautiful little excuse for their behavior—in other words they have learned to lie. Whereas baboons haven't yet learned that.

M: So you're saying that you've learned about people in mainly a negative sense? Meaning that, if we were honest, we would behave more like baboons?

R: But that's not negative. If you take parallels from the goings-on in a baboon troop to what's going on in a human troop—call it a nation—it's exactly the same thing, except that we are such a deceitful bloody species. And you know why? Because we have invented language. We can happily say one thing and mean exactly the opposite, you see. Now I'm not saying that baboons haven't got a language, but they certainly haven't got a language to deceive you with. You always know where you stand with them. And you can take it or leave it.

M: Now wait. I have noticed in the little time I've been here with the baboons that I never quite know what to expect. Of course, when I first arrived and they didn't know me, they would occasionally mob me and the like.

R: You're talking about the little guys now.

M: Yes, the little guys and the medium guys. For example, they will come to me and we will be having a very sweet interaction—lip-smacking and stroking—and then suddenly something—maybe a quick move on my part—triggers a negative reaction on their part.

R: Doing what?

M: Like the two or three times when they mobbed me. I don't know why.

R: They looked into your heart. Have you ever looked into your heart? Were you a bit scared? Were you a bit nervous?

M: Yes, perhaps a bit.

R: And that's why. So they took advantage. If you show the baboons weakness, they will openly take advantage of it. They don't make a sweet story of it: You're scared, and they get you. And then you are number two. End of story.

M: So you think they intuitively pick up what's going on with you.

R: Absolutely. I don't know how they pick it up, but they do. Perhaps it is telepathy; you don't have to say a word. People try to explain it with body language, but I don't think that's it. You couldn't pick that much up through body language.

M: I think it's something almost chemical, since we humans have it, too.

R: So there! Now you're saying it: 'We humans have it too.' Which is why I began by saying to you that, if you want to know what humans are all about, look at baboons. [She laughs.] There is no good reason, when you look at evolution, that we never had it, because we claim to be the most evolved creatures on earth. We just, at some stage in our development, made a horrible U-turn and lost a lot of abilities that they still have.

M: And do you have a theory as to where, or when, that U-turn took place?

R: No. And it's not important. It's just such a pity that we have become such idiots. We have pills for everything; we have medicine for everything; we have an explanation for everything—all that comes from very well-spoken scientists. But when you say to them, 'Please say that in plain English,' they can't. Because they've got to get rid of their big words that mean nothing. It's our fault. If we had the abilities that a baboon has, my God, life would be easy. If we had the honesty, or the guts, to stick to what we believe and say so. . . . You don't have to be rude to do that, yet we spend our lives using beautiful words . . . to do what? To mislead the world. Isn't it so? And those who have perfected it most of all are the politicians. And then you get an old woman like me who speaks her mind and what they say is, 'God, she's just a crazy old bat.' The other kind of response I often get is, 'God, your honesty is very refreshing.'

M: That's a euphemism—*refreshing*. It means you're a bitch.

R: [Laughing] I don't want to be a bitch. I just want to call a fish a fish and a bird a bird and a fact a fact. But we do exactly the opposite—and that's what you call 'smart' today. In my day it was different. We said, 'You're lying.' Today, you're 'smart.'

M: Or *charming*. I've thought about this, since the word 'charm' comes from casting a spell. It's really a kind of negative thing to be charming, isn't it?

R: Yes, of course. *Because* you're casting a spell. You're telling a person exactly what he wants to hear.

M: Now, tell me. I haven't been here long, and I'm certainly no expert on baboons, but if you listen or watch, there's a great deal of play, of hierarchy, of loyalty, etc., in the baboon world, and there's also, within that system, a great deal of conflict.

R: Oh yeah. But very openly. Very openly. They will never hire an assassin to solve their problems.

M: But to take it a step further, do you think that conflict is inherent in human life?

R: The moment a person thinks, there must be conflict. Because we all think differently. And if we really had that spark of divinity that the Bible tells us we have and were made in the image of God, then we should be able to overcome this conflict. And that gives me the best indication that this is all a lot of humbug. We are not made in the image of God! I certainly wouldn't like a God like us! So it's just arrogant to think about our being made in God's image.

M: Do you think, since we are not all alike, that there are some people who are gentler, kinder, more good or evil than others? Or do you think we are all alike? You and I, for example, are certainly not at all alike.

R: No, not at all. But the problem is that we haven't got respect for the differences: We always think we are right. When I was young, people spent a lot of their energy in creating harmony. Today—I was just speaking to Angela [a volunteer] about this—nobody gives a damn about anything until there is a certain amount of money in it. And they won't do anything without a reward. I really have yet to meet a person who does anything without having somewhere in his mind the idea, 'What can I get out of it?'

M: I can tell you one.

R: Tell me.

M: My wife.

R: Then you are lucky. That's wonderful.

M: She's not like that at all. In fact, sometimes I wish she were more like that because then we wouldn't always be worrying about money.

R: It's all very relative, isn't it? You can be very rich without having anything in your bank account.

M: I myself am not such a lover of humanity. In fact, I'm very selective about who I choose to be with, so that, for example, it's quite hard for me to be in a place like this, where I'm just, so to speak, planted in the middle of a 'troop.'

R: So you come back to basics. And how you handle that affects your life. And you have exactly the same thing in a baboon troop. You'll have a male arriving, proudly declaring, 'I am!' and chasing a little female with a baby. And you know what? He's got a hell of a hard time to get to the top. On the other hand, the guy that comes and is nice and says, 'Hey, what a nice baby. Can I come and have a look at it?' By the time he's finished, he's got seven or eight females backing him.

M: So it pays to be charming in the baboon world, doesn't it?

R: Yes, but it's not any kind of an act. It's part of their natural makeup. It's not some sort of role-playing—'I will be charming and then I'll get to the top. ' There really are good charming guys that don't have to put it on. They're born with it.

M: And you don't think the same is true of people?

R: I think it's in a lot of people, but it gets hammered out of them, because from the time they're very small, they're told, 'Don't do that; it doesn't pay.' You see, I've got a lot of young people coming through here that could potentially be fantastic people, and I see them go and my heart bleeds, because I see what's coming: 'That doesn't pay, that doesn't pay, don't do that, there are better jobs than that.' And I sit here and I say to them that if you have a passion, whether it pays or doesn't pay, that will make you the happiest person under the sun. If you've got a passion, you're so lucky because most people haven't got one. It gets hammered out of them. This little Emma [another of the volunteers, a sophomore at Columbia], she's got a passion. I've got a lot of hope for her.

M: I suppose you know, of course, that the words *passion* and *suffering* come from the same root.

R: I wouldn't be surprised. You just have to have the courage to follow it. But most people haven't got that courage because there's somebody standing there with a carrot and a stick, saying, 'If you go that way, there's a carrot; if you go the other way, you can't have the carrot. . . . You get the stick.'

M: But I think that most people have the passion beaten out of them before they even get there.

R: But don't blame whoever beats it out of a person because the moment that person is grown up, she's got herr own mind, and she should have the courage to follow it. I was brought up in a very close-knit family, and one day I looked up and I said, 'No! I won't wear a hat going to work.' 'No! I'm going to work in the zoo, even if it is very disreputable.' In those days, you only had drunkards and the holy eminence working in the zoo, and you wouldn't want to have your daughter seen there. But that's where I wanted to work. So I said to my family, 'Well, it's been nice knowing you.' And I walked away. And that was not done in those days. But you've got to have the courage to do that.

M: I didn't have the courage, to tell you the truth.

R: And did it make you happy?

M: That I didn't have the courage? Of course not.

R: You see. That's why you need to have the courage to go out and do what you really want to do, because whom are you pleasing? You know, Bridget [an eighty-year-old, nearly blind friend of Rita's who is British and lives in Portugal, and who was visiting Rita while I was there], I have a great deal of respect for her, although she drives me bloody crazy. I didn't have to run around with her. It was just that I felt I wanted to. Because she definitely possesses a very special mind, and I've got respect for a lot of the things she does.

M: Do you agree with me—or maybe it's merely my excuse—that one of the main myths we are exposed to when we are young is that men are stronger than women. And yet all of my experience tells me exactly the opposite.

R: You know, I'm sitting here having a look at it, and I say to myself, 'How the devil did men ever get that right?' To maintain that myth. And I don't mean it badly. I just cannot understand how they managed to repress women for so long—and I blame the bloody church for it. And I'm the last person that wants to see women's emancipation taking over. In fact, I feel very sorry for the guys, because I see men today hovering in the corner and terrified and being chased by predatory females. And this is also not how it should be. But the world has always moved from one extreme to another, and that's where we are at the moment; but what can you do when you see things are not working as they should be? Female or not female, I couldn't care a staff, but things have to be done, and if females can get them done better, then let them get on with it. The point will come when men will say, 'Well, what the hell?' and there will be no distinction between the sexes. It will be the better person who eventually comes out on top. And this is a development that we just have to wait for.

It's just as stupid as racism, this male/female thing. I really think it's natural to say, for example, that men have been the hunters, so why take it away from them? They have so much fun hunting, so why must the females do it. [She stops, and suddenly says, 'Isn't that gorgeous? There's a newborn gecko walking along the wall here. . . . Can you see it? '] So I think people should be more relaxed about the whole thing. I think there are basic elements, and that's why I say to look at the baboons, and you would say, 'That's why things happen.' And we have ought to have the brains to say, 'That's why things happen,' and to do it the proper way. But we don't do it.

M: We don't do it because so many people think they have something to lose.

R: Exactly. It's total selfishness. I mean I don't know how you were brought up, but we were brought up that it wasn't smart to be selfish. You weren't supposed to even show that you were selfish, and you were supposed to fight it. I was brought up to take the smallest piece of cake, and the smallest piece of chocolate. Today, you are supposedly smart if you say, 'That's mine. . . . I want more . . . and more and more and more.'

M: I was brought up, on the other hand, with a very mixed message. On the one hand, that you shouldn't be selfish, but, on the other, there was also a kind of martyrdom and self-sacrifice.

R: But it shouldn't be martyrdom. It just wasn't done. It wasn't considered smart to be selfish. We knew we had this greed thing within us, but, being a human being, you were supposed to fight it. Now, for example, some men are very jealous. But that wasn't considered smart—you were supposed to have more sense, and look beyond it. I think now we are actually regressing, I really do.

M: I have the feeling that, when I'm with the baboons and one is starting to get friendlier with me and approaching me, that very often another one will come and push him off.

R: Exactly. Because there's this ranking business going on, and they've got this straight ranking system. For example, if you have a fight in a baby cage, we want to step in and punish the one that we think is wrong. But that's not what you do with baboons. You never stop the fight. What you do is you take the fighter in your arms and you love him. And then you switch him around just like that. He becomes the sweetest thing. You see what I mean? Doesn't that teach you something? It is something that is contrary to how we feel, but that's how it's done. And these are basic, basic reactions.

M: But we also know, for example, that the people who lash out the most tend to be the most wounded people. If you take the extreme, say Hitler, clearly somebody capable of such evil had to have experienced great suffering, don't you think?

R: Well, the big thing about Hitler is that he was a silly little man. And now they are trying to make things out of him that I think he doesn't even deserve to be credited with. I think he was a silly little man who had a lot of charisma. I saw him once, and people were going crazy, and I was convinced that there was something wrong with me. Because I looked at him and I thought, 'Gee, he's much smaller than I thought! Why is everyone going crazy?'

I was only eight or nine years old. It was mass hysteria. I could never even understand him when he was making his speeches—he had this awful Austrian accent and I didn't know what the hell he was talking about. But everyone screamed and shouted, so I thought there was something wrong with me.

M: When I was a kid, I was utterly fascinated by him.

R: I was never *fascinated* by him. But I liked being a Nazi because I liked competition; I liked sports. I liked to be tops in all sorts of things, and that's how he captured children. And that's all. I had a bloody big problem because I wasn't the tallest—I was always third in the row when we had to line up in groups of five—so I became a leader so that I could pick my team. It was all a competition thing, which I liked, because I was good at things.

M: Do you have brothers and sisters?

R: I have one brother who was born after the War. I don't know the guy at all. He came visiting here just recently. I think it was just before you came. I hadn't seen him in twenty years and I said to Lee [her assistant], 'I don't know what to expect.'

M: You had the same parents?

R: Yes, the same mother and father.

M: And what happened?

R: We just went separate ways. I went to Africa, and he did his stint in life, and we could have been strangers. I had no particular reason to like him; but I said to Lee, when he came, that I was pleasantly surprised. And the only reason I could see why I liked him is that he spent five years in the desert. That is what shapes people— going into nature and back to basics. And there you go—five years. And I quite liked him. I liked what I saw. Not because he was my brother, but because we both spoke a sort of similar language.

M: And where does he live now?

R: Still in the desert . . . in Namibia. Digging for diamonds on the Skeleton Coast. And this, I think, is part of our family. You know what he said to me? He said, 'I think the Neumann family is partially crazy.' And I said to him, 'I agree with you.' And he actually found diamonds, after everybody told him he was crazy to look for them; but now he wants to get out of it because the whole business thing is too much for him; and he wants to sell it. And I told him, 'Good idea.' His daughter was brought up as a Jehovah's Witness. And he said to me, 'You will never guess what Eureka [his daughter] is doing?' And I said, 'No, tell me.' 'Well,' he said, 'she's gone to India and she is swallowing fire and swords in a show.' Now if that's not crazy, you tell me what is! And he's very proud of her. And he walked out of here and he said, 'Well, I'm glad you're a Neumann.' Which shows me I'm mad. And I said, 'Well, I'm glad, too.'

M: And that was the first time you'd seen him in twenty years?

R: Yes. I actually thought that he was in trouble, because I'd seen him once or twice years ago when he was in trouble, but not otherwise.

M: Let me be honest with you about something. You make me jealous. You know, I would like to be more like you.

R: [She laughs.] You can be like me.

M: Okay, but let's not be silly. I can't simply wake up one morning and say, 'Okay, no more Michael Blumenthal—I'm going to be just like Rita Miljo.' Look, you're here; you're trying to raise and nurture these baboons. You're trying, somehow, to rehabilitate them, to give them back what their mothers didn't give them.

R: They're the last creatures under the sun that nobody cares about. That's why.

M: Is that how you explain it?

R: How do you explain having a passion?

M: But why do you think so many people care about other animals on the African continent, and no one else about baboons.

R: Because of the personal glory that goes with it. I think that ninety percent of the people who care about animals do so because of the glory. Most certainly . . . and the money that goes along with it today.

M: I think that what draws people to an animal is that they feel some sort of identification with it. For example, I don't really like dogs—your own dogs are fine, believe me—but I generally prefer cats.

R: I don't think you make a decision. Either you like animals or you don't. I'm not terribly fond of snakes, for example, but I think all the animals are put into our care. And a dog, for example, lives to make you happy. And *you* don't like him for it?

M: Well, actually, that's a bit of what I don't like. A cat, on the other hand, has the same need for me that I have for the cat: none.

R: True. A cat can live very nicely without you, thank you. We had feral cats here, and people wanted to shoot them. And I said no. They are sitting there because people just didn't look after them. But they have absolutely no inclination to mix with humans.

M: I've often been to the zoo, and I've noticed that, whereas people love to go visit the chimps and gorillas and orangutans and other monkeys, they don't, generally, gravitate toward the baboons.

R: No, not at all. Because the baboons are always holding up a mirror to them, saying, 'Here, this is you.' And people don't like that.

M: Probably you're right. But then I look at someone like you, and I say to myself: Here's someone so straightforward, so without bullshit—how did she ever get to be that way? And I then think to myself, well, she must have somewhere had parents who really supported her, no?

R: Not really. I hardly knew my father, as I told you. He went off to the War, and then he came back and I hardly knew him. He was a stranger to me. The only time after that I really came to know my father was when he was dying of cancer and I spent six or seven weeks with him, thank God, so that I have very fond memories of him. Otherwise I couldn't have cared less. My mother, well, she was a very pretty woman. She spoiled me, but I don't really think my mother had very much influence on my life. My grandmother, she was very loving. HERE

M: Well, I think, I suppose, that we are like the baboons in that we learn from, and mirror, our surroundings. A baboon, for example, will learn from the alpha male, or from an alpha female, how to behave, how to groom, how to eat, etc. . . . No?

R: They have an etiquette and a way of doing things that could be written down, and they live with only that. Everything is prescribed. And within that system they have to develop their own way to outsmart each other. Otherwise #5 would always get the last of the food, one might think, but if she's really smart, she might get more than #1.

M: But, you know, we humans also have a system. For example, I once went, after twenty years, to my high school reunion. And what was very interesting was that you see these people that you haven't seen in decades. And in high school so-and-so was a king or a queen because they were pretty and athletic, etc., etc., and so-and-so was a nobody. But now, that person who was so magnificent in high school has turned out to be a nothing, and the little ugly one in the corner is a world-famous biochemist or cancer researcher and has suddenly become, in an unconventional way, highly attractive.

R: Because the insignificant people, like the baboons, have to work that much harder to get ahead. If you have daughters, for example, the pretty ones are always the problem, because they think all they have to do is smile and everyone will fall at their feet. And the ones who are not so pretty really have to work hard to get what they want.

It's also in part a question of how you grew up. I grew up thinking I am the ugliest thing under the sun. And I look at pictures of myself now from when I was younger and I think to myself, 'Well, you really weren't that bad looking.' But I don't think it did me any harm, because I really had to work at being noticed, because I thought I was not pretty enough. And the pretty girls said, 'Well, I've got it all made.' Even though they were pretty dumb upstairs.

M: When I was in high school, we had this category called 'Most Likely To Succeed.' But it was never the one who was voted Most Likely To Succeed who actually succeeded—it was always some idiot that no one much even noticed.

R: And that's what makes life really interesting. The only time I was really unhappy in this life was when my husband was making so much money. It took all the joy out of my life. That was my only really unhappy time. But otherwise I must say that I had ideas of what I wanted to do in my life, and I've done them all. Yes, I think I've done them all. I never wanted to do bungee jumping or things like that.

M: All right. So you say you had an idea of what you wanted to do with your life, and that obviously meant having something to do with caring for animals, right?

R: Yes, but I think you're born with that. I remember my father was that way too. It was before the War—I was seven when the War started—and I remember that every Sunday he used to take me on long walks through the forest, and that stuck with me.

M: You mean looking at the animals and things like that.

R: Yes. Because he loved animals, too. And I think you're either born with this or not. And my mother wasn't quite like that. She didn't quite say no, but she didn't like me bringing frogs and rats and things like that into the house. But my father was actually the inspiration for that sort of thing. And I think you're either born with it or not.

M: But you just contradicted yourself. You said you're born with it, but then you also said that you got it from being with your father.

R: Yes, but I think it was actually the genes that came through, you know.

M: But then I look at my experience. I grew up with a father who did not have my genes. He was not my biological father.

R: Yes, but you might have gotten the genes from your grandfather or grandmother. That's always part of the mystery, no?

M: Yes, of course, but you're always fighting this battle of whether it's nature or nurture: Is it the genes or the experience? Because the father whose genes I had was a chicken farmer and a fighter. He even had a bullet in his arm from the Israeli War of Independence in 1948. I still remember looking out the window as a child and seeing the bullet glistening in the sunlight. Now, he was a completely different man from the father I grew up with. *That* father was a salesman and a flatterer of women who was always trying to sell something to someone. But to tell you the truth, perhaps unfortunately, I got more from the father who raised me than from the father who made me.

R: Look, I'm not just talking about animals. Like my husband, he came from a very small farming community. His father and mother had a small family farm. But where did he get his genius from to become such a wonderful engineer? It must have come from somewhere, certainly not from his parents. He most certainly was outstanding in this respect—not idiotically scientific. He could just take a look at pages of figures and say, immediately, 'Look, that's how it works.' And his colleagues would spend days looking at the same figures, filling pages and pages of paper with calculations, and finally come back to him and say, 'You know, Lothar, you're right—that's how it works!' And my husband simply responded, 'See, I told you so.'

Now I think you're either born with that or you're not. Nobody can teach you that.

M: Of course, there are certain talents that are gifts. Music, for example, is most certainly a gift. I always tell my poetry students that the most important gift a poet has is a good ear for language, for the way the language sounds. Now, you can work at that—you can try to get it by hard work—but you will never have it the way someone who has an innately musical ear will have it.

R: You either have it or you don't, that's what I think, too. How can you possibly sit and cogitate and make a poem? I find it really difficult. I really, for example, loved Rainer Maria Rilke when I was young; I really loved that guy. And then people translated his poems into French and into English, and I thought: How the hell can you guys do that?

M: You know what the poet Robert Frost said? 'Poetry is what is lost in translation.'

R: And that is how we learned Shakespeare, too. We translated Shakespeare into German, and I hated that. And then I read the original Shakespeare and I thought, 'This is beautiful.'

M: Well, you know, I must admit that, although German is my mother tongue, I am very lazy about reading in it, and when I first read Rilke—even the *Duino Elegies*, for example—I read it only in translation.

R: You did? Poor you!

M: Yes, but I must admit that, even in translation, they are still very beautiful.

R: Well, maybe someone had the same feelings as Rilke. But Shakespeare's stories in English shook me to the bone. Shakespeare in German is absolutely terrible!

M: Yes, I can imagine. I myself once saw *Hamlet* performed in Hebrew in Israel, and I must confess—though the only Hebrew I actually know is prayer-book Hebrew—it struck me as terribly strange, and rather awful.

R: Listen, I came to South Africa and at first I was missing my culture. And someone said to me, 'You know, at the Opera they are playing Figaro's *Hochzeit [The Marriage of Figaro]* at the moment. So I went to the opera and there they were, playing Figaro's *Hochzeit* in Afrikaans! And I was on the floor laughing! It was, of course, more than comedy; it was ridiculous. Can you see what language can do?

M: So what about culture? What would be the baboon equivalent of culture?

R: What would any animal do with so-called culture, tell me? It's totally useless in their life. All they've got to do is try and survive. We made ourselves the masters of the universe so we could afford to have culture. Whether it is any good for us is another story.

M: I ask myself the same question, to be honest, because I myself am supposed to be an artist. But sometimes I ask myself, 'Does the world really need this?'

R: Well, if you are an artist you will touch people who have similar feelings to yours, whether you are a painter or a writer of poetry or a musician. You strike a chord with similar minds. And that's what, unfortunately, gives you the money. If you strike enough chords, then you make money. If you don't . . . well, then you have a problem.

M: Yes, that's true. But I, for example, have never really tried to strike a large number of chords. I simply wanted to strike the ones that really mattered to me, to affect those who were, or are, my kindred spirits.

R: But the animals have one question only, and that is to survive. And they can survive without a poem [laughs], usually.

M: And that, of course, is the human condition for those who are more or less well enough off. We spend all this energy creating conditions in which we no longer need merely to survive, and then what do we do with the excess energy we now have?

R: At the moment, we create diseases.

M: Yes, we create diseases, we write poems, we create complicated love stories, and, unlike the baboons, we don't stick together; we aren't loyal to each other; we don't expend our energy the same way the baboons do.

R: Because that is only neded to survive. And because we don't do that, we will not survive. We will only kill each other and destroy each other. And unless somebody can get through to people's hearts and say, 'Look, that's what you're doing,' we're going to destroy ourselves. That's the bottom line of it. So what do you want to do about it? Maybe it's a good thing. If you have a body full of cancer, it is a good thing to get rid of that cancer; and at the moment the human race is a cancer on this planet because they are so totally, totally selfish. There's nothing else but themselves, and then themselves again and then themselves a third time. And who are you? What do you want? Just go away!

M: The Russian poet Joseph Brodsky used to say that the great tragedy of human life was that the power of evil was greater than the power of good, that evil people have more force, more energy, than good people. And I think, in a way, that it's true. I know a lot of good people. If, for example, the world were full of people like my wife—as I said earlier, she's a far better person than I am—we wouldn't have problems. She doesn't care about money; she doesn't ask what's in it for her; she doesn't behave that way at all. But she's also a person without any power in the world, except in her small sphere, which of course is important—she works in a hospice center with dying people for almost nothing. It's like what you're doing here. You can ask yourself—Is it going to change the world? Well, absolutely not.

R: Absolutely not. Just look at all the energy I've had to expend to fight. Look at all the fights I've had. Unbelievable fights. For what? To save a couple of hundred baboons? It is, from the collective point of view, a waste of time. But okay. Now take any other kind of person, for example, who goes to the stock exchange and makes so many thousands of dollars a month.

M: A day! Even a minute!

R: Yes, say a minute. So what has he achieved? It's all relative.

M: Of course. And this I'm sure of: The only thing we can really do in this life is to make a dent. If the dent is 600 baboons, fine. If the dent is one child who feels good about himself and is loved, fine. It doesn't matter. I believe that the goal of human life is simply to be better than what made us, to somehow give better than we got.

R: Well, better or worse, that's relative. But I think that if you're prepared to give—to honestly give—even if it's wrong, you can never go wrong. And most people don't even dare to do that.

M: I think it's partly because instead of being respected in this world, they are mostly mocked for it, mostly belittled.

R: So for that you need a strong mind. When I think how they mocked me, how they couldn't look past my madness of trying to look after baboons. And you know what I said? I said, 'Go and get stuffed!' And thirty years later they don't mock anymore. Well, I'm glad I lived that long. But who cares? Who really cares? When you think about whose opinions you depend on—and that's a good thing about getting older—you really couldn't care less about the others. You know that you're sure of yourself, and you really couldn't care what anybody else thinks. When you're young, you try and please the world until you realize that the world is really a bunch of idiots. And that is the liberation you have when you are old. That's why I thoroughly enjoy being old. [She laughs.]

M: Yes, it's a big advantage, I know. But still it takes a lot of courage. Because when you're out there in this world—maybe not in this room, but in most places—every signal you get is the opposite: that it's good to be selfish, rich, acquisitive, famous, greedy, and narcissistic.

R: You know what? I still remember the time when that was not so, when those were dirty words. So we can either hope that everything goes in a circle—that we will come back to the place where those are once again dirty words—or that it will destroy us. Which, then, is what we deserve.

M: How did you feel when that baboon died today? [A baboon had died earlier that day from the lethal bite of a black mamba snake.]

R: I have seen so much death in my life and yet it still affects me very very badly. Any death really gets to me. But then, you don't really know who's next. What can you say? There was really nothing that I could do. If a mamba walks through the cage and gets him, what can I do?

M: Of course. And this, as you get older, is something you also have to accept: that life contains suffering and pain. And you can wish until you turn blue in the face for goodness to prevail, or for an end to suffering, and sometimes it just seems there is little you can do about it.

R: There's quite a lot people individually can do, but sometimes people would just rather look the other way. But that is for them to work through.

M: Yes, but it still takes courage. And I really think, in general, that women are more courageous than men are, at least many of the women I know.

R: I learned one thing in my life that is really a huge positive thing, and I learned it when my husband and daughter died. I was able to close the door and say, 'Well, I will look at that tomorrow,' because I knew that I couldn't cope with it today. And if you can do that, you can overcome these things. Otherwise they just take you down. But that's discipline, I think. And that's one thing that I think Hitler taught us [laughs], a means of survival. And some people are strong and some people are not that strong; it's an individual thing.

But whatever you look at, once you get to be my age, it's such a sad thing to see everything being destroyed and dying around you; but that is what this world is made of. You can't stop it. It would be nice to see something improving, but you look at science, for example, and I remember when my mother was dying of cancer, we did everything we could to keep her alive because we believed that the cure for cancer was just around the corner. God almighty, that was forty years ago!

M: But a cure for cancer is one thing, and the cause of cancer is another, isn't it?

R: Yes, sure. But then you have this bloody scientist who sends me an e-mail about wanting to study geriatric baboons as a way of improving on Viagra instead of doing something that would improve the world. That's what I'm questioning, and you can understand my anger.

M: I'm amazed that people aren't angry all the time. When we learn that in the United States, one percent of the people possess sixty percent of the nation's wealth, you would think there would be revolution! But practically no one gives a shit. And you know why? Because they all hope, somehow, that one day they will be among that one percent.

R: But things are changing, and they are changing very much the way I saw them change during the War. Because they go step by step, really, and we live in a very frightening time. I don't know how it is in America, but here in Africa life is very cheap. You can die for a toy or a cell phone. And nobody is really upset about it. You either adapt and live or you don't adapt and die. People don't care whether you live or die.

When I came to this country and there was a person lying on the road, everybody would stop and say, 'My God, can we help?' You go to Jo-burg today and see whether if there is a person lying on the road anybody would stop. They will look the other way and think: don't get involved.

M: I notice that, even in Hungary, if someone falls in the metro station, people rush right over to help and see what they can do. But that hardly ever happens in the States. People are too afraid to get involved, I think, myself often included.

R: And so if that's the way we're going, that's what we're getting, and that's what we deserve. There is nothing much more you can say.

M: I remember once when I was young and very worried about my father, who had a bad heart. My father came home from work one day and told me he had stopped to help a man who had fallen on the subway platform, and then, when he left the station, he realized that the man had stolen his wallet!

R: Not only humans can be that tricky. I have seen a crocodile, hiding down by the river, camouflaged in the bushes, just waiting for a little baboon to come by so he can go and grab him.

M: Yes, disguise and deception, just like we use. It's a big question, the relationship between human life and the state of what we call 'nature.'

R: There is nothing really good about nature. Nature is very cruel. We will never be able to live like that, but somehow I think that the basics, which are nature, give you some cleansing inside, and you are able to sort out what's important and what isn't important, so that you can get rid of the unimportant things.

M: But everybody has to do it in their own way. For example, I come here, and part of me is terrified: It's new and not at all the same as being in my garden in Hungary where an occasional hedgehog comes along. Here there are animals that can kill you!

R: Well, of course it's all new to you. But what you have to learn after a while is that there is no such thing here as killing for the fun of it. A lion will eat you if he's hungry. If he's not hungry, he'll walk straight past you. There is nothing but necessity involved in it. And what I try and teach the youngsters who come here is that you actually can live in nature peacefully, if you respect it. There's a spider right there. It's actually not pretty, but it's quite okay. So why kill it? It has the same right to live in nature that we do.

And once you have that attitude, the animals pick it up. I remember when I first moved here, and there was a lot of shooting and running around. And I was like a little ship, and everyone just came and sat here until the weekend was over, including the baboons. They pick it up. They pick it up, and they won't harm you . . . unless, of course, they're really hungry. But there is a reason every time you get harmed. Basically, it's because you don't realize what you're doing. But we really shouldn't be that stupid. We have that superior brain, remember?

M: It's quite simply a very different kind of life here.

R: It's a totally different life.

M: I remember when I was a kid in the Washington Heights area of New York, a neighborhood filled with German-Jewish refugees. And there were only two kinds of animals—mice and roaches. And what did we do with them? For the mice, we baited mousetraps with cheese and killed them. And, as for the roaches, I would go into the kitchen at night, where they would be running around the stove, and I would turn them on their backs and light their legs with a match! Because we thought of these animals as dirty and disease-producing and disgusting.

R: A roach is actually one of the cleanest creatures. I don't really like them either, but what can you do? I have owned this place now for forty years, and twenty years ago there were so many animals, so many insects, that you practically couldn't get into your own bath. But you know what? Now that's all gone. It's a frightening, frightening thing, how all those creatures—even the little creepy crawlies—are disappearing.

M: And why is that?

R: Now you tell me. You tell me. Normally, when we were sitting here, like you and I are doing now, there would be so many frogs shouting outside that we probably couldn't have understood what we were saying to each other. Where are the frogs? You would go out, and you couldn't even get outside because of all the bats. Where are the bats?

M: I must confess that I've seen quite a lot of bats since I got here.

R: No, you just see the odd bat here and there. You have no idea about the insect and small animal life we had here that has just quietly disappeared. And why? Here, for example, you're not allowed to use poisons, since you might poison a cockroach, and then that cockroach will be eaten by a squirrel, and the squirrel dies. But there is something going on that nobody takes note of. I got an e-mail just the other day saying that fifty percent of all the bees in the States have disappeared.

M: Yes, I've heard reports about that as well.

R: And Einstein once said that if the bees all disappear, people will have just three or four weeks to live. Just work it out. It's the bees who are the pollinators of everything—ninety percent of it is done by bees. And if we have no bees, we will have no grain, no fruit, no corn, no anything. But people don't care. And then they say, 'Oh my gosh, what are we going to do now? Eat our money? Or our cell phone? Or what?' And then you have bloody scientists who are saying, 'But we knew nothing about it!' Nice, eh?

M: I must tell you, though, that these kind of matters—global warming, for example—are getting much more attention, at least in the States.

R: Okay, so take climate change. Remember that they laughed at us for years when we tried to talk about it. And what did Bush have to say? *Nothing*, until he got hit with Katrina, and then he said, 'Yes, of course we've got climate change, does anyone have anything against it?' Well, what does he think—that we are stupid?

And then they have it all worked out beautifully, that we have a trade in emission capacity. Okay, you don't use all the emissions that you've been given—can we borrow some from you? Thank you. And that will certainly improve the planet, won't it? Are they crazy? Who do they think they can bulldoze, tell me?

M: Well, I also think this is partially because we have no sense of ourselves in time any longer. It used to be that people had a sense of themselves within some continuum of history and time. Now, we only have one moment in time: the present. We don't even stop to think about the future.

R: Then why do I get a lot of young people in here who are not like this? Look at little Emma, for example—she is a gem, an absolute gem, and she's also living in America. So why isn't she like that?

M: Well, I think it's because, gratefully, the spirit wants to reassert itself. But unfortunately, so many people's spirits are completely crushed and overcome by the crude materialism of what's around them.

R: But why do they allow that to happen?

M: They allow it to happen because they're weak, or aren't aware of the fact that there are alternatives, because they've grown up with parents who imitate that culture. There are all kinds of reasons, and some people simply don't have the courage to say, 'This violates my spirit. This makes my soul sick. This is not what life should be about.' A lot of people simply don't have that courage.

R: They used to. They used to have the courage. But where, today, are the great minds? Where are the Goethes and the Schillers? We don't have that anymore. We just have a bunch of people going yeah yeah yeah, and jabbering about. We don't have any leaders. That's our problem. Everybody needs a role model. Who are our role models? These funny idiots from Hollywood who adopt babies by the dozens? Just find me one! I would be very grateful.

M: In the United States we have some courageous and straight-talking people. Like Noam Chomsky.

R: Who is he? Never heard of him. Why haven't I heard of him?

M: You haven't heard of him because the mainstream media rarely mentions him, or people like him.

R: And whose fault is that?

M: The fault is with the world of money, with who controls so much of what we see and hear, especially in the media.

R: And who owns the mainstream media?

M: Well, the large business conglomerates. People like Rupert Murdoch and Ted Turner and so on. Why, every night we are subjected to some serious-faced news anchor giving us the world's famines and tragedies with a grim and compassionate face at a salary of millions of dollars per year. How are we supposed to take any of that seriously? The fact is that those good people we are talking about do exist, but that it's difficult to find them unless you search search search.

R: So what I'm saying to you is that we have the wrong leaders.

M: Well, of course we have the wrong leaders. All you have to do is think about the enormous amounts of money they have to raise merely in order to run for office, and you can see why.

R: For example, who is this funny little Black guy who is now running for President.

M: You mean Barack Obama?

R: Well, who gives him money in order to run?

M: The people who have it, of course.

R: Yes, and then they call in the chips and say: This is what you owe us. But why do we tolerate this? Why don't we fight it? If I were young . . .

M: Yes, if you were young, what would you do?

R: I would fight that big time. Maybe I would be another Bin Laden. Just look at his story: They call it terrorism. The guy has got ideals. Why would he go kill people otherwise, unless he had ideals. He hates America. And he did a bloody good job with this 9/11. He needed brains for that. And he frightened the pants off of every American. For years now, we have a war in Afghanistan, we have a war in Iraq, and we use that as an excuse to climb into everything where there is something to be had—oil or diamonds or what-have-you.

"Bin Laden is a terrorist, and if you don't listen, he might get you." And everybody is frightened to hell. But haven't they deserved what they get?

M: Some people—even some public intellectuals such as Susan Sontag—actually voiced similar sentiments after 9/11, and they were utterly condemned and ostracized by most people.

R: But what makes Americans think that they are so untouchable? Millions of people in Africa starve to death or get killed. And they couldn't give a staff, because there is no oil. And then he kills 3,000 people in the World Trade Center, and the world has to stand at attention. Who do they think they are?

M: It often comes down, quite simply, to who has the power. There was an American philosopher, Emerson, who once said that God's law is that you can have power or you can have joy, but not both. Which is what I've been saying to you: that people who have power and cultivate power and care about power are generally not the kind of people who bring joy into the world. They bring death.

R: They don't even bring joy to themselves. Instead, we have here in South Africa an ocean of people who are scared shitless to do something about this. For instance, people are here complain about Zimbabwe, and an 86-year-old man [Robert Mugabe] running that country, and there's not one who has the guts to take a gun and shoot the bloody bastard and put an end to it. You tell me: Don't they deserve what they have?

M: Well, I think that everyone has some place in their life where they have, or need to have, courage. And I don't think it necessarily needs to be some dramatic or large event, either. There are many small acts of courage that go unrecognized in people's daily lives that may, in the end, be at least as worthy as shooting a dictator.

R: Yes, but he can't be dislodged otherwise. So shoot the bastard. It's his time to go anyway.

M: I do remember asking my father when I was young, 'Dad, why didn't anybody ever shoot Hitler?' One guy, of course, did try.

R: Yes, but that was a bad situation. It was a bungled-up attempt.

M: Still, you think: Here was a guy who killed millions of people, who thrust the entire world into an awful World War: Couldn't somebody have gotten the job done of killing him? But who do they kill instead? Gandhi, Martin Luther King, the Kennedys. It's the good people who get killed. Does Idi Amin get killed? Does Mugabe get killed? Of course not.

R: So what does that tell you about the human species?

M: It tells you, once again, that evil seems to have more power—or at least more courage—than good. Good people simply don't take guns into schools and shoot people, in general. There's an American priest, who's also a poet, named James Kavanaugh, who has a book of poems entitled *There Are Men Too Gentle to Live Among Wolves*, and I think that title tells us something rather true: Most good people are not people who kill people, or want to pull triggers, or make war.

R: Well, if I had to solve one of my situations, and nothing else would help, I would be prepared to take my gun and shoot him. And I wouldn't feel bad about it. If you've tried everything in your power to do it the proper way and nothing's working, and you really feel the necessity that he shouldn't be there, well then you've got to have the guts to do it.

M: Logically and factually speaking, I think you're right. All one has to do is consider how much bloodshed and tragedy might have been avoided by killing certain individuals.

R: But then you've got to have something that sustains you. Look at all these suicide bombers. What sustains them? Their belief. They're prepared to blow themselves up, not because they want to kill five Americans and twenty other people. They do it for their God, which is just as stupid. What if he's not there, and the whole thing is a sham? But that's how you get to people.

M: But these people also usually come from the most despairing and economically deprived classes. They are not people who have good lives that are worth staying alive for; so it's rather easy to recruit people like that, I think. It's a bit like Bob Dylan said, 'When you ain't got nothin', you've got nothin' to lose.' And it's a bit like that.

R: But going back to our baboons, I think that we are on the top of the primate ladder. And the higher up you go, the more emotions you have to deal with. Baboons have basic emotions. But just take people—my God, we've got it all! Bloody stupid, huh?

M: And do you think that baboons experience anything like what we call love? I mean, they obviously experience tenderness.

R: Just watching them, living with them, I notice a lot of feeling and emotion. But for a long time you couldn't say so because, for example, my friend, Professor Handy [Charles Handy, specialist in organizational behavior], was saying, 'Don't talk like this—you'll lose all credibility.' But now the circle is coming around. All of a sudden, animals are seen as having emotions, and I'm reading this book called *Baboon Metaphysics* [U of Chicago Press, 2007], and guess what they come up with? And you say, 'Why not?' I mean the baboons most certainly have got their own choices and guys they don't like that much. And hostility. And there are definitely lasting friendships—especially between female and male baboons.

M: Which last throughout their lives?

R: Yes, for a long time. And I think that is a huge field of discovery that we still have to go through. And now they don't frown upon it anymore. I mean people throughout history have always had this question about what do animals feel and what do people feel, and of course through the Church's influence there was this large gulf established between animals and people, because *we* were made in the image of God and animals were made to serve us. You could even eat them and sacrifice them and burn a thousand of them for your sins.

And so it was a long road to overcome all that. Now, when I look at what people are researching, I laugh, because they are fundamental, stupid things. You know the truth if you *feel* for animals. I never subscribed to all these beliefs that animals haven't got any feelings and they haven't got any emotions and they can't think and they can't recognize. I mean, what kind of an existence would that be? I'm even convinced that trees can cry when you cut them down.

There are a lot of things we don't know, and the scientists, over the last fifty years, have discouraged us from investigating this kind of thing. It mostly started with Darwin coming up with his theory of evolution, and there were a lot of really bitchy scientists with their theories who wanted to bite each other's heads off. And until recently, you weren't supposed to say, like I do, that I have a sort of an understanding with them, like with Eule [one of Rita's older baboons, a member of the wild troop]—she *tells* me things, like 'Get me a banana,' and I get up and I do what she tells me; and there she is, waiting for her banana. And I think, 'How did I get here?'

But you tell this to a scientist and he'll say, 'Don't ever tell that to anybody. . . . That is senseless.'

M: Yes, of course. Because a purely rationalistic mind can't let in that kind of information.

R: I've also got a very interesting story with twin baboons—something I'd never heard of before. And we took them away from the mother because the one—the little one—was only half the size of the other.

M: Now, when you say twins, you mean that they were not just siblings.

R: No, I mean twins. In all the many years I'd been working with baboons, I'd never been able to record, or see, the birth of a new one. It happens very, very fast. And one evening the volunteers up in the mountain lodge called me and said, 'You must come—there's a baboon giving birth!' And I ran up, and she was giving birth to *two* babies. And when you see them today, you cannot tell them apart. You could at first, while one was much smaller, but now that one has caught up.

M: And where are they?

R: They are with one of our foster mothers in Jo-burg.

M: And how old are they now?

R: They were born about three months ago. They will be coming up to live here in another month or so.

M: So that must be really rare—not just a double birth, but twins!

R: I had never heard of that before. If we had not come across her giving birth—the second one was half the size of the first—by the time we went to look for them in the morning, we would have seen the first one, but we wouldn't even have found the second. But as she was giving birth to the first one, I was watching and thinking that we've got to make sure that the afterbirth is coming out. And then another baby came out!

And there she was holding this whole bloody mess—the afterbirth and two babies. She was obviously confused. She didn't know what to do. And the bigger one, of course, grabbed her, and the smaller one was only able to grab his brother. She tried to clean them, and then the little one fell down. And obviously she couldn't carry the two of them at once, or she didn't realize that she had given birth to twins—I mean she's not meant to have two babies—so I rushed into the enclosure and I picked up the little one, and then I put my mattress there and I thought, 'Now I'm going to watch this.' And there was so much confusion that I realized I'd have to pull them both out of the enclosure.

So I got Stephen [the release manager] to dart her, and I got the other one out. And it was very strange, because normally baboons grab each other and hold on. But, here, the two babies didn't want to be together. I couldn't even put them in the same box! But now they are inseparable, and the older they get, the more they look like twins. There is no doubt about it.

It will be totally interesting to see how their life will now go—whether they will stand up for each other, or whether there will be some kind of special bond. That's a very interesting thing that is coming our way!

M: So you're quite sure they are twins.

R: Very sure. But there was a guy on the Cape who phoned me and said he had heard we had twins. He wouldn't believe me when I told him it was true. I asked him if he wanted to do a DNA test, but he never phoned back.

But they would never have survived if we hadn't taken them. The mother wouldn't have been able to cope. It's a little like the Cain and Abel story—one always is defeated.

M: I'd like to talk a bit about the baboons' habit of grooming. I called my son yesterday and said to him, 'Well, about an hour ago, a baboon was grooming my neck, another my hair, another was cleaning my ears, and the other was grooming the hair on my chest.' And he couldn't believe it.

R: You know what? You must actually enjoy that. If you go in, for example, with Fila or Olive—I've got to sort Olive's cages out—they groom you, and it is *sooo* relaxing. The little ones, you know, are really not proficient in grooming properly. They try, of course. But the older females—my God! They are so good at grooming that you ask yourself, 'Why did we humans ever abandon that?'

M: I'll tell you a rather intimate detail about my marriage, which is probably a bit indiscrete of me. I myself am a bit squeamish, but my wife loves to look on my back for various skin imperfections—I won't go into the gory details—and to push and prod and pull and put everything in order back there. A kind of grooming, I suppose, no?

R: Yes, absolutely. And, you know, grooming is terribly important in a baboon's life—and it's *not* looking for fleas. They come across external parasites, yes, but baboons as such never have fleas. If the little ones do have fleas, then you can be sure that they were somehow together with dogs; and you will see the groomer take the flea, look at it, and do this [flicks with her finger], and the flea jumps into their face! So that is really not the idea of grooming. The idea is to relax you, and to make you feel part of the group.

M: Yes, and it feels like a very professional hairdresser is working on you.

R: There've even been scientific papers written about who grooms who and why, and of course in true human fashion there has to be a *reason* why they do it, and we assume they are waiting for reciprocal favors, and every bloody reason, you know. But when you watch them at the beach [along the Oliphant River, on Rita's property], they always adopt a certain pose: 'Okay, I'm ready for grooming. Anybody here?' And you see the females move up and do that, but the grownup males never reciprocate in grooming unless they are in a consort situation where they want to mate with the female. *Then* they sit and groom the female.

M: So for the males, it's only if they're going to get, so to speak, a reward.

R: Yes, absolutely. And of course the females lap it up. They think it's wonderful. But basically if you deprive them of grooming, it's a very cruel thing to do. When they are under stress and there isn't enough food, so that they have to spend all their time trying to get a bit of food into their stomachs, they haven't got time for grooming.

M: They seem to groom a bit the way Gandhi used to weave. He used to do that as a kind of meditation activity when he was under great stress.

I now also know exactly when the baboons wake up—at 5:57. I hear them come down from the trees onto my roof, and then I begin to hear *their wa-hooing* and copulation cries.

R: You know, that alone shows you how wrong scientists are when they say they don't know what they're doing, because they get up, they make their noises to chase everything else away, but they don't then go and wander off into the blue yonder. They have *destinations* to which they go in the morning. And at this time of the year, and a bit later when it's colder, they sleep in the big trees, and the first thing they do is they get off their cold trees and go up into the hills and wait for the sun to come up. And then they get the first sunlight, and they get warm.

And, for God's sake, they obviously have enough brains to say, 'I'm cold, I'm going up the hill, because that's where the sun comes up.' You don't think that they wander around blind until they find a warm spot!

M: Well, they are certainly very smart—and they also love to figure things out, like untying my shoelaces. Sometimes I try and hide the ends of the laces, or make some tricky knot—but they always figure it out.

R: If you have that Velcro on your shoes, they really love that!

M: Why do the baboons off in the distance sometimes make so much noise?

R: That's usually the troop sleeping in the big tree down by the river, or it might be some wild troop about two kilometers off. Somebody may be hunting them. Perhaps a leopard.

M: Do the leopards ever come up here?

R: Yes, sometimes, though rarely. But then, of course, if there's a large shouting match, the leopard will think once or twice before getting into the middle of that. That's why they're shouting. They don't have an easy life.

M: It's not just a joke when people say it's a jungle out there. It really is! But it's clear to me that you prefer baboons to humans, isn't that right?

R: Yes, definitely. At least I know where I stand with them.

M: Isn't that because they are less complex than we are? They have a less complex brain, and a less complex evolution; that they are simply *simpler?* They may be more 'honest,' as you put it; but they do not have a brain, history or environment that is as complex as the human one. I simply don't think it's quite comparable. It's like saying that we're not like a turtle! It's not comparable, is it?

R: Why does everybody harp on the subject? You are compared and forced and expected to love humans, and only *then* can you care about animals!

M: No, I don't agree with you there. You're not compelled to love humans first—and perhaps humans need the protection less than animals do. But I just think that, in a way, if you dislike your own species, how do you go about explaining that you yourself are a part of it?

R: Well, I don't even quite know why you want to go down that road. I mean, everybody does strange things in this life.

M: That's for sure . . .

R: And if somebody goes and says, 'I prefer animals to people,' well, we've got a good reason today to do that. I've come across this so often in my career: 'Why don't you rather look after orphaned children? Why don't use that money for something else?'

M: But I don't agree with that at all, nor would I ever say that to you. I think what you're doing is remarkable, and I think that anyone who saves *anything* living is doing something great, whether it's a tree or a flower or a garden or a baboon. So that's not my point.

R: So then what is your point?

M: The purpose of my question is certainly *not* to say 'Why baboons and not children?' The purpose of my question . . .

R: [Interrupting] Why don't you go to a priest and ask him why he became a priest? He'll give you a wonderful sermon to tell you how much he wants to save your soul, and how much he wants to do this and that for you. Well, you'll never hear me saying that about the baboons [laughing]. I mean, human beings explain themselves in the most rosy way, you know? I don't know why I like baboons, but what I've been going through with human beings all my life doesn't endear them to me. I'm perfectly happy without them.

Whenever there were television shows or something like that made about me, I would say, yes, well I prefer to work with baboons, at least I know where I stand; people lie too much. And, my God, I was ostracized for the next five years! Be my guest—I don't mind. But you know, if you say to a person, 'I don't like you, and I don't like you because of this that and the other,' that person doesn't look at himself and say, 'Well, maybe she's got a point.' They turn around and say, 'Well, what an idiot!' and then they find another reason why I am an idiot. Which is much more complicated than turning around and looking at yourself and saying, 'Well, I wonder what it is that she doesn't like about me.'

You don't make choices with living creatures who suffer because of your choices. You can't do that. Just as much as you can't—you shouldn't, though they do it now—in the hospitals say, 'Oh, I can't treat you now, because you can't pay me.'

M: That's utterly immoral and disgusting. And I know that it happens.

R: I mean the basics are the same.

M: But maybe you still have to ask yourself, 'What will enable me to do the best possible job with these baboons? At which time will there be a point of diminishing returns?'

R: So then you can go euthanize them ... but you have to live with it. That is what IFAW [the International Fund for Animal Welfare] once suggested to me: 'Don't take any more.' And I just walked out of that meeting. Because you're talking life there; you're talking destiny. And you just go and euthanize because the numbers don't gel anymore? You can't do that. And who the hell are you to play God as to who lives and who dies?

You know, you came at a very unsettled time here. When you walk away from your empire and you see it crumbling, that's not so good, is it? Basically, I can't have the opinion that there is nothing that can save this planet and then try and save baboons. It's like the case with that little piglet [warthog] we had to euthanize yesterday—decisions have to be made.

M: You mean that little one that was in the cage?

R: Yes. I mean, we could either have amputated its leg, and then it would be eaten by lions in the first week; or we make it easier for him and let him die peacefully. And that's what we decided to do. We really tried so hard for this little guy. We just picked him up and thought we could make a difference ... but it didn't work.

M: But, I think that's part of what heroism is—and part of what makes *you* heroic. You do something *despite* the fact that you don't have great optimism as to he ultimate outcome. What other choice do we have? *To do nothing?* And I feel the same way about having a child. You say, 'Why have a child when there's no future and the planet is going to hell?' Of course you have your selfish 'hormonal' reasons. But you also do it in the hope that it can make some small difference in the world.

Well, there's a great deal to human emotions. And I don't think we can ever really understand another human being completely . . . not even, or perhaps least of all, ourselves. Why, you can live with someone for twenty or fifty years without ever really understanding them, don't you think?

R: You know, that's what bothers me. I had a few shocks last year where I had a really high opinion of two people—I would have gone through fire for them—and they just showed their clay feet. After twenty years of knowing them and thinking there are straightforward people. And then you think to yourself, 'What was I, stupid? Or what?'

M: There are very few people in the world, I think, Rita, who do not have within them somewhere a core of weakness.

R: Then they should at least have the honesty to say, 'Yes, I'm weak.' That I can accept. But to still insist that they're right—that I don't accept.

M: I myself am very hesitant to judge other people, because I myself don't know how—under certain extreme situations of stress or danger—I would react. I often ask myself, for example, how I would have behaved in the camps, or how I would have behaved under Hitler if I had been a German. And I would be lying if I said I am certain that the answer would be all that flattering to me. It's difficult, I think, to judge people fairly or accurately.

R: You know, judging and being disappointed are two different things. If you expect certain things from a person and he or she doesn't do it, you are totally disappointed and you may turn your back on that person. That doesn't mean you're judging him: you're just practically judging your own judgment.

M: Yet I think that, in the end, people are just trying—in ways that are often actually quite screwed up and perverse—to survive, just as the baboons are. They are trying to survive by making a living, by educating their children, by protecting their families, by getting a woman or a man. And I think that, behind it all, much like the baboons at times, people feel endangered—that they are simply trying to make it through the day in the best possible way they can.

R: Baboons are the perfect stealers, but they steal in order to have food that directly goes into their mouths—not to pile it up somewhere and say let's count the money later.

M: But they also sometimes feel in danger, don't they? Let's say by an alpha male who walks into the cage—or by a human male, for that matter.

R: I don't think so. I think it is always about food, basically.

M: Food and sex, no?

R: Yes [laughs] . . . sex plays a big role in it, too.

M: And that's, in part, what I think money has become in our lives—a kind of substitute for food and sex. People deal with money in a very primitive way.

R: Yes, but they should know better. That's why we've got these superior brains, no? But I don't think we'll ever solve it. It will be interesting to see what becomes of the world.

M: Yes, you think about it a lot when you have a kid.

R: That's what I said to Angela [one of the volunteers] today: 'Don't even dream of having a kid. Don't be crazy. You don't even know whether you have a planet for your kid. Why would you want to have a kid?'

M: Well, but look—the baboons all want to have kids, no?

R: Yes, but I don't think there is that much thought, or emotion, behind it, since the only animals that actually grieve are the elephants.

With baboons, it looks, from our point of view, very touching when a mother loses her baby and carries this dead baby around for a week, but I don't believe she does it out of emotions. She is just not aware of the fact of death, and she carries it around until she realizes this is not a child anymore, and then she forgets about it. It's just us with our super-emotional things that make big stories out of it.

M: I actually have a poem in one of my books, called "The Elephants Dying," which is precisely about that—how touching it is when the elephants return to the bones of their dead to mourn, how deeply moving.

R: And yet animals most definitely have a sense of bonding. I remember the lions that I brought up. There were the two boys, brothers, and there was a hell of a bond between them. When I moved them from here, because they needed better places, we had to dart them. So we first darted the one lion and, just by accident, the dart hit a vein and, as it hit the vein, he just fell over, as if a bullet had hit him. And the brother rushed over and stood over him, so that there was nobody getting near him. He was protecting that seemingly dead brother of his. And there were a lot of people here observing, and there was just dead silence. And I said to them, 'Yeah, and you want to tell me that animals have no feelings!' It was unbelievable to see that. We had to dart the other boy, and he fought—like a lion!—and he fell on his brother, so as to protect him. It was unbelievable! He thought his brother was dead.

So they have those feelings, you see? Maybe when I look at the baboons and I see they are really not that affected by death, I look at it as one of those kindnesses of nature. But every human being thinks that they are immortal. Like look at me: I'm nearly eighty years old and I've got plans for the next five hundred years! Like there is no fright or anything. Oh my God, I could die any night of something! Because that doesn't happen to me. And I think that the baboons have the same feeling: Death doesn't happen to them. And so it is actually a gift of nature to allow you to go on.

You know, we always see these sob stories coming up, like when someone is diagnosed and is told, 'You've got three months to live.' And, my God, the only way we really go on as if we were indestructible is when we don't know.

M: The poet Stanley Kunitz, who died not long ago, once said that the most important fact of his life was that he was living and dying at the same time. Which, of course, is true of all of us. I myself am aware of it every day—that it could go on for another forty years, or that it could be over at any moment. And here [laughing] I'm particularly aware of it—that, if one of those black mambas crosses my path in a bad mood, it can be over in a second!

R: But maybe it's a good thing, you know?

M: And, since I like so much to quote lines from poets to you, I'll quote you another, this one about death from the British poet Philip Larkin: 'Most things will never happen,' is what he said about death. 'This one will.' But let's hope not tonight. . . .

R: Well, it's got to happen sometime, no?

M: Yes, but better later than sooner, I think.

R: Which is why I end up spending time with someone like Bridget. I just wouldn't want to end up like her—with such an active mind and unable to do anything any more. And you have to depend on other people—that must be dreadful!

It's not easy to spend a day with Bridget, because she's got a mind like mine—'We'll do this and this, and such and such, and not that.' And the only way she softens things is by throwing this word 'Darling' in between, which makes it a little bit softer. But what she says has to be done! Which is why I feel so particularly sorry for her now, since she has to depend on people. Why, she was sitting there yesterday and she had to pack her things, but she couldn't see. And so I packed up her things for her and counted her money, and I thought to myself, 'My God, I hope I never have to do that!'

M: I can't remember who first said it, but it's true: Growing old is not for sissies.

R: My grandmother was totally deaf. And she got bitter and twisted because she was sure we all made jokes about her. And that really wasn't nice—neither for her nor for us.

But I myself feel good when I meet a person with whom I feel I have something in common, or I meet someone to whom I can truly give something. Look, I had a hard time with Bridget, but I felt glad that I could help her, and I have a feeling that she appreciated it. And there was no ulterior motive. I understand her madness. And I was glad to be able to do that, because maybe I will never see her again. But to do that makes us understand that we probably need this crowd around us, and that we were not meant to be on our own, you know? Otherwise, how could people manipulate us the way our politicians do?

But we run in a crowd and we all shout the same songs, and then we step back and say, 'Are we mad to do that?' But there is something in us that needs it. And if we would simply give people a little smile in the morning or something like that. . . . For example, Bridget was totally bowled over when someone said to her, 'You really look charming today.' Now, there was nothing charming about her, but she had tried so hard to look her best.

M: But wouldn't you also say, 'Now there's someone who is insincere, who didn't say what she really meant?'

R: Well, I don't know about insincere. That person was simply acknowledging the fact that Bridget made the effort to look like a lady and to wear lipstick, etc. Now, if you ever see me wearing lipstick, then you know I am ready to do something really drastic! But, for her, it was merely a recognition of her efforts. It doesn't really cost you terribly much just to be nice. And people don't really do that anymore—and that is thoughtless and selfish, I think. But I think we need it anyway. If I go to town where every goddamn bastard knows me, and I say, 'Hey, I need this,' and someone says, 'Well, sit down, I'll do it for you,' I say under my breath, 'Thank God,' and I feel good. And I don't think that they're being insincere.

M: You can be a person who gives something to others without being insincere, I think. Just as you can have emotions without being sentimental. It doesn't mean you have to become someone else's dishrag. Like you, for example—I certainly don't think of you as a sentimental person, but I think you are very feeling-full.

R: I think that old people are sentimental, but they usually keep it to themselves.

M: Hitler, they say, was very sentimental. Why, he listened to Mahler and Bruckner and treated his German shepherd quite wonderfully, while at the same time he was sending millions of people to the ovens.

R: Yes, but he didn't do it himself. He just signed a piece of paper.

M: That's very easy to do, isn't it?

R: Yes, that's very easy. But you remember during the war what the Bund did by throwing bombs on those small towns? They had no idea what they were doing on the ground.

M: Just like the so-called 'immaculate bombs' we dropped on Kuwait and Iraq during the first Gulf War. General Schwartzkopf would come out there and show the press these immaculate little arrows that were actually bombs being dropped and killing people on the ground.

R: What really got me were the trials that they ran to judge all the people—the commandants and so on—who actually did all the work in the concentration camps. That's hands-on; that I couldn't understand, how anybody can do that. There were children there—how could you do that to children? You know, I don't even want to think of it. How could anyone do a thing like that?

M: But I think they are almost less guilty than those who merely signed the papers. Because you could sign a paper condemning millions of people to death—men, women, and children—and you would never even have to see the results of your signature, or face the physical consequences of what you were doing.

R: I don't agree with you. When I stopped being a Catholic was when they started telling me about hell and purgatory. I looked at it and I thought, 'Well, I'm cross with my dog, so I'm going to take the tail of the dog and shut the door on it. And the dog will howl his head off for eternity. And I will sit there and I will say, "You know what? That serves you right." I couldn't do that even for a minute—and God wants to do that to us for an eternity? You can have your God, you know? But you've got to do that yourself. It's another thing to read about it or to sign a piece of paper. It's one thing to really see a war first hand, and another to start a war and sit in Washington. They don't know what they are starting.

M: But ignorance too can be a terrible crime. It's so easy and inviting to be abstract. The vegetarians, for example—rightly, I think—argue that people eat meat but refuse to go out and do the killing that allows them to do so. But somebody had to kill that cow, somebody had to kill that chicken, and so on. Are the rest of us so innocent, compared to the actual killers? I don't think so.

R: It's funny that you say so. Because I also stopped eating meat when I started going to the *abbatoir* to get food for my lions, and I saw what was going on. And that's the same thing—I saw what was going on.

I would really like to know what Hitler might have said if someone had taken him and stuck him right into the middle of a concentration camp, and said, 'Here, you do the gassing today.' That's what I would have liked to see. Because I really think that the guys who did it, hands on, were the bastards. For him, it was a political thing. My problem with Hitler was that he wasn't really very intelligent. If you want to run a country and you start a war and you see that you're losing that war, you don't just go and kill another couple of thousand of people. You say, 'We've got to stop it—we've lost.' Isn't that so? But of course, he didn't do that, and that was totally unintelligent.

I mean look at bloody Bush. What he did for America you can never repair again. He started it on the way down. And America will be the next country and continent that will go up in flames, just like Russia did. And he'll go home to his Texas ranch and say, 'Well, I had a good time for eight years. Now you can do what you like with the mess I left.' And nobody hangs him. And nobody says, 'Well, you are responsible for that. Now pack your bags and go to Iraq.' And let him fight.

M: And do you think there is one member of the American Congress with a child in Iraq? Only one, in fact—and he was elected long after the war had begun. The others are sending mostly the children of the poor and uneducated to Iraq to die.

R: It was exactly the same here when they sent all these young soldiers into Namibia, and to fight in Angola. And I said to the guys, 'Are you crazy?' And, my God, they looked at me and said, 'How would you know? You are still a bloody German. You don't understand.' And now look at them today—'Why did my child have to die there?' I warned you. I told you it was a lot of shit.

M: If we only had a law that everybody who votes in favor of a war or starts one would have to send their own kid, we wouldn't have any wars. What makes so much evil possible, I believe, is that it's so often abstract. You are doing everything at a distance.

R: Any politician who starts a war, you should put him in his underpants and let them fight it out. And then we'll watch who wins— and we wouldn't have any wars! [Laughs.]

M: And that's precisely what makes so much evil possible, the fact that's it so often abstract: You're signing papers; you're dropping bombs from thousands of feet in the air. It's easy. You show up at Wahnsee, and say, 'Let's kill all the Jews.' You have some nice euphemisms for the killing, sign the papers, provide an official stamp— wham bam! That's it.

R: But then look at it. They always have to have somebody whose fault it is. In Germany it was the Jews; in America now it's Al Qaeda . . . has the pattern changed at all?

M: You always need a bad guy. You need someone to blame.

R: And you need the people to be scared of something.

M: This was the genius of the psychologist Carl Jung. He knew that what we are really most afraid of is our own shadow—the parts of ourselves that are too frightening, or unflattering, for us to claim, and which we then project on others. So . . . I think, in fact, that you're doing quite fine here. You're doing the best you can do.

R: Well, you know, you have to eventually be the bad old bag, but what else can you do? You know, we had this young guy here, who put together a wonderful poster about snakes and reptiles in this area. I'm very proud of this youngster. His father phoned me—a man from Greece or Turkey or some rather obscure place—and he said, 'My son is dropping out of college, can he come?' And everybody was up in arms, but I said, 'Sure, let him come.' And the kid has so much going for him; he is so filled with enthusiasm. It's just unbelievable. What a lovely boy he is!

M: And where is he now?

R: He's at the Waldorf College here. And he said to me, 'You know, we have to educate these guys about snakes—we can't just go and kill all the snakes.' And so I said, 'Okay, do it!' And so he did—and he came back to me and brought this poster. And he's only eighteen or so.

M: To change the subject a bit, what did you think of Nelson Mandela? You liked him, didn't you?

R: Yes, he's special. He's in this book about us [picks up the book]. He came to one of our baboon releases. He is a gentle person, he is a nice person, but he's actually a lot more frail than people show him to be. And he has this thing about him to try and say something nice to everybody. He was sitting on one of the cages, and I tried to open the cage, and he said to me—and me being an old woman—'Come here. Does your mother know what you're doing here?' And I felt it was so sweet—why should he do that with an old woman?

I was actually blessed to meet a lot of very special people. Our veterinarian, for example. His father was the third black vet in Africa—what a special guy he was!

M: He's no longer alive?

R: He died in a car accident.

M: You don't know the South African writer, John Coetzee, do you? He's a marvelous writer who won the Nobel Prize several years ago.

R: I've heard of him. When did he get the Nobel Prize?

M: Oh, I think it's about three years ago now. But the reason I bring him up is that he writes a great deal lately about animals, and about the cruelty humans inflict on animals. I think you might like him. I'll send you some of his books when I get back.

BOBBY AND OTHERS

Do you think, by the way, that one day I could get a picture of you with Bobby?

R: Why Bobby?

M: Well, because Bobby was the first of the baboons you brought here—so you kind of started the Center together, no, along with your assistant, Bennett?

R: Well, Bobby is my friend, you know, but I'm not her boss.

M: So I guess we'll have to ask her?

R: And she's such an old cantankerous bitch right now—just like me. It's a question of who's going first. Whenever I go past there and I talk to her, she answers me. But when she's in a bad mood, not a sign. And then I think, 'Oh my God, she died!' But I look again and she's on her elevated bed, and she lies there and she looks at me. [Laughs].

M: And she's always in there alone?

R: Yes, well that's a proper granny cottage she's got.

M: And what about all the others who are in cages alone?

R: They're all males. We keep them there so they won't keep breeding. And also, if they are in an enclosed area and there are big baboons, and there is controversy, such as fights, and they are outside, they can run and can hurt themselves, but not if they are in the cages. So it's for their own protection.

M: And what then happens when the troops are released?

R: They are all released with them. They all go out together.

M: What about the males in the cages alone farther up—like Winston?

R: You mean in the Nut Village? Those are all research baboons. They were used for research like into asbestos dusting. Can you imagine? For thirteen years—just crazy!

M: Speaking of research, one of the things that has most struck me here is the amazingly rapid way in which the baboons heal. It's really utterly amazing. For example, Zefferelli, who broke his arm just the other day, and was back in the cage with his bandage an hour later, acting as if nothing had happened. Someone must have done some research into how baboons—their bones, their wounds, etc.—heal that quickly, right?

R: No, my God! Why should they? That would be bad for the pharmaceutical industry.

M: I've sometimes thought I would like to send my son here to you for a couple of weeks. It would be great for him, though I think he would want to run right out of here the very first days. He's even wimpier than his father is, at least in some areas.

R: Oh my God!

M: Pretty bad, huh.

R: Yeah, but you know what, Michael, I have hope for you. You're just not staying long enough. But most people are sorry when they leave. Only in the fourth week do you realize what it's all about.

M: I know that in myself there's a tendency when I'm confronted with something strange and uncomfortable to want to run. My first instinct is to take off.

R: Well that's a survival instinct.

M: Yes, probably, but I don't think it's always a good one. Because very often, if I can't run and have to stick it out, I find out that it was, in fact, a good experience. But I also think that the ability to do so is something you either get, or don't get, very young.

R: You know, Michael, that's one thing I don't buy from you. It is such a modern thing today, you know, when your life isn't right, when you're a little bit screwed up, the shrinks tell you to go into your pre-vious life, and they say, 'Well, you must have been abused as a child.' And when you say, 'No,' they tell you that it's only because you can't remember. And one thing I truly believe is that no matter what you've had in your previous life or what happened to you, you come to a point where you use your own brain and you work through it and you analyze it and you say, 'Okay, that's where I am now, and how do I go on?' You can't blame all the things that you left behind, because now you're here, and you're you, and you can change your life and behave according to what you want to do.

If you don't do it, it's a weakness of your present state of mind, and then you live with it. I'm not saying that you've got to do it. But if you don't do it, then don't blame your past—blame your present mind that can't deal with it. And these total excuses that they throw at you these days: It is never your fault! You were either abused or this or that or something else. This is a lot of baloney because, let me tell you, I went through each and every thing. I should be so screwed up that I should be locked up. You deal with it when you come to it. And then you make the best you can out of it. And if you can't do that, it's not their fault—it's your fault then.

M: I mostly agree with you, and yet I don't feel it's the same for everyone. You know, insofar as affirmative action goes in the States, they used to make this analogy: There's a mile-long race, and one person starts off with a heavy set of weights tied to his legs, and the other has only his sneakers on. And then, after a half mile, they take the weights off the first person and say, 'Okay, you're equal now—just keep running.'

I do think that sometimes people's lives are a little bit like this. You can catch up, of course, by running a little bit faster, and trying a little bit harder; but the playing field will never be level. I think there really are people—people with lives far worse than yours or mine—who enter life with this weight around their legs, and they don't run the race with the same ease as the rest of us.

R: And I believe that they wouldn't have run the race the same way even if they didn't have the weight. It's a question of the mind. Not everyone will make it. There will always have to be one loser. Isn't it so? I mean, I've seen this country under Apartheid, and there were guys like our Ntiti [the black vet], and he became a vet in spite of the Apartheid regime. And he worked for it—he fought and he bitched and he became a vet. Of course, he was just an outstanding person. He could have sat on his backside and bitched and complained and acted like a victim. But he didn't. That's what makes a person special.

M: That's absolutely true. And that is what makes you special. Why, for example, did some people emerge from the concentration camps and become humanitarians and helpers of others—people like Bruno Bettelheim or Victor Frankl—and why did others become embittered or commit suicide? How do you explain it? You can't.

R: You can't explain it. And it is not just the concentration camps. Some people can deal with bad times in their lives and some people can't. And I am of the opinion that if you go through a really bad time—and I think I had bad times in my life—you can gain a great deal from it. Because I've had such a lot of experience I wouldn't have had in five lives. And I look at these youngsters today, and I think about what I had to do when I was eighteen, and I feel sorry for them. And I think, 'God, how long will it take you to have that bit of experience? You won't have it before you die if you go on like this.' Most people are afraid—they just are too molly-coddled.

M: Well, I'm sure you know what Nietzsche said: '*Alles was mich nicht tötet, macht mich besser*'—Whatever doesn't kill me makes me better.

R: And I think that's one thing that Mandela got: He has no hate in him. And he sat there in jail for twenty-seven years! And he dealt with it, and he understood it, and it made him a better person. And that is the special thing about him. I mean, he's got a totally Afrikaans personal assistant, a woman—she doesn't even hardly speak English.

Now, a lot of people would say, 'You shouldn't even speak Afrikaans, or have anything to do with them.' And yet he's totally comfortable with her—unbelievable! You know, he is such a special person.

M: It's no easy thing not to react to hate with more hate.

R: Yes, and I look at myself, and I see a special fault in me. Because I have hated twice in my life so badly that I could have killed. And to this day I'm not sorry about it, and if I would have had a gun, I would have killed the bastard. That was basically a big fault of mine—I'm not a Nelson Mandela. I have had differences with people that I could sort out after twenty years by them simply saying, 'You know what, I'm sorry.' And I just melt. But those two guys—give them to me now and I would still kill them! It's crazy, isn't it? [Laughs.]

M: I myself am not at all like Mandela. I tend to be someone who loves and hates. And I also tend to feel a bit like the poet Robert Frost, who said that we need hate in order to counterbalance love. It's not something I particularly like about myself, but it's simply the way I am.

R: Mandela, you know, is not a totally intellectual person. When he was young, he liked the ladies, and he still likes the ladies. But when you compare him with all the other idiots who shared the prison with him, nobody else is good enough to even give him a glass of water.

M: Yes, he's very special indeed, almost saint-like. But then how do you explain it? Some people simply don't seem to have this capacity to hate and to hold grudges and to be mean to others. We certainly don't have enough such people in the world, that's for sure.

To change the subject a bit: It occurs to me that you have had the experience of living in the two most infamous racial states of the 20th century—Nazi Germany and Apartheid South Africa, right?

R: Well, actually what happened here was just a copy of what happened in Germany.

M: You think of it as the same?

R: The same. . . . Except here they didn't manage to start a world war [Laughs.]

M: They also didn't exterminate the black population. But, to be frank, when I come here now—and I don't pretend to understand very much about the South African situation—I see you, the white European woman who is the head of the manor, so to speak, and then Lee, another white woman, who is your assistant. And then I see a lot of young black men and women doing very menial jobs around here. And from a very superficial point of view, I try to understand what I'm seeing. For example, if you just put me down here as if I had gotten off a spaceship, I would say that this looks to me like that kind of situation—like Apartheid—still.

R: What do you mean? Are you objecting that we don't have— What do they call it in America?—*affirmative action?* This [she holds out a piece of paper] is affirmative bloody action. And they send you a piece of paper to tell you that next month, every week for one day, they are going to shut your electricity down. Nice, huh?

M: And why are they doing this?

R: Why are they doing this? Because they've got a goddamned bloody blackface running the thing—and he has no clue what to do! So you want to know what affirmative action does to this country? If they've got the brains to do it properly—with pleasure. I am color-blind. To me it's a question of brains. And if they can't do the job, I'm sorry—they shouldn't get the job, regardless of their color.

They're doing it with every bloody thing in this goddamned country. They're even prescribing how many black people have to be on the rugby team! Now, what does that have to do with sports, you tell me? If someone can do the job, I've got nothing against it. But this whole idiotic system that they've got here now is nothing but Apartheid in reverse. I cannot see why a child of fifteen, sixteen, seventeen now has to pay just because he has a white skin. You tell me.

M: But that's exactly the argument for affirmative action—that those white children have already been advantaged by their historical situation.

R: So if they've got the brains, let them sit on their bloody backside and learn. And then they can take over, with pleasure. But they must not go and push the whole country into something that doesn't work, just because they're black.

M: I must play devil's advocate for a moment. Take you and me, for example. We came from basically middle-class families, and had good educations, plenty to eat, etc., etc. The argument is that the blacks here in South African began the 'race' with a weight on their legs, and . . .

R: Now wait wait wait a minute. I disagree with you here because the blacks here in South Africa had a better educational system under the old government than they have now. The only thing that they complained about was that in the schools—and that didn't only go for black schools, that went for every school—the teaching was done in Afrikaans, which was the worst possible tool you could give anybody. And that disadvantaged not only the black people, but the white children as well. You could only insist on an English school if you could prove you had English ancestors. Otherwise you were stuck with the bloody Afrikaner school.

But the system worked! They had decent teachers. Okay, they had to make the effort to get to school—but that's always been there. Today, they don't have an education system anymore. What they have done is that they have so lowered the standards that every idiot who can manage to write his name will get matriculated. And then their guys get out and want to take over jobs. Do you really have to know what you're doing? And it doesn't work.

M: But what do you do, really? I ask myself: What do you do if one people have been historically and systematically repressed by another? Of course, we had slavery in the United States, and many black people grew up in truly disadvantaged situations.

R: But they're doing it, and nothing has changed! Do you think that when I came to this country I perpetuated Hitler's policies and only had white friends?

M: Of course not.

R: I had all sorts of colored friends. And that was against the law, and I told them loud and clear, 'Get out of my house! It's my house and I can do what I like. And if you don't like it, go speak to the German consulate.' And they left me alone, you see. You just had to put your foot down.

But the point here is that I would not feel comfortable ever if I were to get a job or anything else just because I was the right color. I do not think it does any good that people get stuck on a rugby team and they cannot play rugby, but they've got to have five blacks on the team. If I would be that person, I would say, 'You know what? I don't want to be on your team.' What good does it do an unqualified black person if now everyone who starts a business has to have a black partner? He's nothing but a showcase! And what is the attitude of those people? Have they got no backbone? Have they got no pride? They know they can't contribute; they know they are stupid; they know they can't do the job, but because they have a black skin—pay out. What good is that?

I'm looking at the development of this country, and there is really not much of a black middle class. You've got the bloody fat cats that earn millions, and then you've got the poorest of the poor. There's nothing in between. It may have something to do with the fact that it's also in the way—I don't know, I hate to have to call it culture—in the way their minds work. You know, you've got the Germans, who are always busy little bees and who want to work, and they're not happy if they don't work. A black person is perfectly happy if he's never going to work in his life—if you give him so much a month and he can sit on the stoop and drink.

M: Well, I don't think it's fair to say *a* black person—it's *some* black people, and it's some white people as well, no?

R: No, no, no. I mean, if you live in Africa, that is the general attitude of black people, because only black people live here. And they will never understand why we are such busy bees. Never, you know.

M: On the other hand, look at the Chinese people in many places, or the Koreans. It seems to me, in many places I've lived, that they show up, and within a few months they have a restaurant or a grocery store, or they have a business.

R: You would never see that happening with a black person. Ever. I mean, when I came here, the only ones who had these cafés that were open twenty-four hours a day, seven days a week were the Greeks. No Afrikaner would have done that. It doesn't matter whether they were white or black. They would have said, 'You must be joking!'

M: But what about the black elite who made their way into prominence? The Nelson Mandelas and the Bishop Tutus and the Woye Soyinkas? They're different, aren't they?

R: I don't think they're different. They were just lucky. I've known Tutu from the beginning of his career.

M: And . . .

R: And it's opportunity. But then you don't have to be black, white, or yellow. People are smart today if they can work as little as possible for as much money as they can get. But, again, it's the attitude.

M: Well, look at Barack Obama, this half-black young guy who's now running for president in the United States. He's an incredibly enterprising and charismatic person.

R: That has nothing to do with color. You've got enterprising people in every world, and everywhere. How do you say in German?— *Die Ausname macht . . .*

M: The exception proves the rule.

R: Yes, that's how it is. I personally look at it this way: There are too many human beings in this world, and so we have to have some mechanism to thin ourselves out. And the mechanism is nationalism, xenophobia, and all that kind of thing. After the last war, we all wanted to be world citizens, and the last thing that was in fashion was nationalism.

But now, please, just look at Germany! If they could, they would go back and have their own Bavarian kingdom, and their own Austrian kingdom, and their own Prussian kingdom, and what have you. We've just completed the circle. In Africa it's even worse, because every little bloody tribe has got their own chief and their own language. So, for God's sake, there they sit and they are the best of all and they've done that for as long as you can think the guy next door had to be killed. The chimpanzees do it—nothing new. It's just a question of too many creatures of the same kind. So there must be a mechanism for thinning them out.

M: That may be true. But life was also simpler in many ways when people did not so easily travel and relocate and mix with each other. Being a German, for example, was simpler before there were Jews and Turks and all that.

R: But the Jews in Germany *were* German. It was only Hitler that turned it around. They were more German than the Germans.

M: And Hitler taught them that they were not.

R: It's funny, because he, Hitler, would be thriving today, with all the DNA research. My God, he would be happy, wouldn't he? [Laughs.]

M: Because the biggest human problem is simple dishonesty— that people simply refuse to call a spade a spade and a heart a heart.

R: Exactly. You know how I am—I speak my mind. And I have never had a problem with any black person in talking straight … never. Because they know where it comes from, and they know I mean it. End of story. But you can make a big issue out of what I say if you take it out of context and say, 'That's what the white people say in South Africa.' It's ridiculous.

M: But that's because you actually have courage. It takes courage to treat a black and a white person as if color didn't matter. So many of us whites, when we are with black people, have almost an automatic reaction to be a little more deferential, a little bit more careful, to watch what we say. It's not a good thing to do, but we've been trained to do it, or told to do it, and it's very difficult for many of us to simply behave, as you suggest, in a colorblind way.

R: I can understand that. I think because of my own training, and because of my having been brought up by and under Hitler, I lean over in the other direction—that what's got to be said is being said. Never mind on whose toes I tread.

M: It's the ultimate equality to be treated that way, and I think it's completely right to do so.

R: But you know what, Michael, I basically get on very well with the black people here. Because they know what I say—even if they don't like it—because they know that I'm trying to be fair. And they trust me in that respect. Because they have qualities that we have lost in our smartness. You know, they still have certain ways that we've discounted, and you can appeal to those ways. So I get on very well with them because they remember my values. I find it much easier, for example, to deal with baboons than with white people. Because at least in a way they take it one step further. With the baboons I always know where I stand. With the black people I most of the time know where I stand. But, crap, give me these educated white people and I have no idea! That's what I'm saying.

M: That's because you are direct and honest—you're not a bullshit artist. You say what's on your mind.

R: But what's the point otherwise? Why do people do that?

M: Because people are frightened.

R: Of what?

M: I'm not really sure. A lot of these possible solutions to social problems are not the kind that 'nice' people would like to hear. But perhaps, at a certain critical point, they are the only possible ones that might work.

R: They immediately get out of hand when they are put into the control of a person who has too much power. It's very difficult to implement.

M: And then, in the extreme, you wind up with a Hitler, or a Mugabe, or an Idi Amin or Saddam Hussein. All in the interests of making a 'better race.'

R: I don't know what really got him [Hitler] to do that. I really haven't sorted it out yet. I think it all started with the fact that, if you want to get to power, you've got to find somebody to blame for your misfortunes. I mean, it's the same thing that you've got in America now. You've got to kill Al Qaeda—the terrorists. You need somebody to blame. And I think that, on the same level, Hitler blamed the Jews because they happened to be the rich people. You know, it's very easy to do that. I mean, the pattern is exactly the same.

M: Well, in the United States, a number of people increasingly argue—and I consider myself among them—that rather than having color-based affirmative action, if we are to have affirmative action at all, it should be class-based. Because it's class, rather than color, that is the real disadvantaging factor in society.

R: Probably you're right, yeah.

M: You know, Rita, I have been almost everywhere. I've grown up in a ghetto without English, I've gone to an Ivy League law school, I've taught at Harvard and at all kinds of poor and less prestigious colleges all over the world, and, though I may not know that much about race, I do know a lot about class. And class makes such a difference in peoples' lives.

The students I taught at Harvard were a good example of this. So many of them grew up in families where their parents taught them everything about wheeling and dealing and making contacts and how to get ahead in the world. My parents, on the other hand, hardly even spoke English, and could give me nothing on that front at all. Or I look, even more close to home, at the difference between me and my son, because I, too, am now of at least a different educational—if not economic—class than my parents were.

And it is not all equal. So how can you suddenly say—as if it was Day One: Now the playing field is equal; now everyone has the same chance? Because it's not true.

R: Yes, it's not really true, and it never will be really true, and you will never be able to implement it. People get to places, or to positions, through their own efforts, and they have been able to do that under the old government in South Africa very easily. I have had a lot of very intellectual black friends, and the whole world was shouting their heads off that there is no opportunity for them to learn. That is a lot of nonsense. They didn't have it as easy as the white people because they had to fight for everything, but nothing stopped them if they had the drive.

M: But was it as it is in the United States? In the States I have friends who are middle-class black intellectuals, but they mostly came from middle-class families. Wasn't that also true here?

R: Not as markedly, for sure.

M: Do you know that in the original Constitution of the United States, a black person, for the purposes of voting, was considered to be three-fifths of a human being?

R: And what about females? They didn't have the right to vote either?

M: No. It was even worse for them—they didn't have the right to vote at all!

R: Because the men had a rib missing, right? [Laughs.] But isn't it all terribly ridiculous?

M: It's not ridiculous for the people who are on the bottom. I think that, fundamentally, you can have two possible attitudes. You can, on the one hand, simply say that life is unfair, period, and accept it. That it's a jungle—a bit like a baboon troop: The strong survive and become alphas; the weak have to live as well as possible. The difference, of course, in the baboon troop is that even when the weak get attacked, everyone else bands together to defend them!

You can either take that attitude, or you can try and adopt another attitude: How can we make this very unfair life somehow a bit more fair?

R: If that is what you are wrestling with, there is no such thing.

M: It's not possible?

R: There is no such thing? My beloved Doktor Politz [the Jewish principal who came back after the War] comes in. She came to Germany from America in 1945 and we were all horrified to hear that this Jew came from America to take over our school, and we thought that we were all going to be hanged and quartered and poisoned and what not. My God! And we watched her like a hawk. And there she was. And she couldn't have cared less. And she just carried on. And we sat back and we watched her some more, and we watched her some more, and we thought, 'Well, this isn't possible!' And by the time we looked up, we had more respect for her than anybody could have ever beaten into us.

M: It's like the Mandela situation. He emerged from twenty-seven years in prison on Roberts Island, and one would have thought that he would be vindictive and hateful and . . .

R: And the very first thing that woman told us was, 'Don't be fooled by the democracy.' I mean, we came out of the Hitler thing and there was democracy. And she said, "No no no no no! Let's talk about this."

M: And what did she mean when she said, 'Don't be fooled by democracy'?

R: She actually gave us the ingredients of democracy and we said, 'Now, we haven't established that—that's not the perfect way of ruling a nation!' And she demonstrated that very, very quickly. And then she said, 'Now, let's think about that.' And we struggled with it. And we tried kingdoms and Kaisers, and we tried chiefs and we tried everything; we tried priests and so on. And we thought about it, and we asked, 'Now, what would be the ideal government for human beings?' And we actually came up with the idea that the ideal thing would be . . .

M: A benevolent dictatorship.

R: Yes, a benevolent dictatorship. And then we said, 'Okay, which human being is benevolent?' There is no such thing, so we will always have a faulty government.

M: The best quote about government and democracy, I think, comes from Winston Churchill. He said, 'Democracy is the worst of all political systems . . . until, that is, you compare it with every other system.' What's the alternative?

R: But look at it. Democracy for Africa is a total bloody disaster. Because of ignorance. They have now tried the—whatever it is—to elect their president. You know how it takes place? On the grounds here. And we are in what they call a Plattland—that means in a tribal, simple-minded area. And the candidate, who's an ANC bigshot, he hires a truck and he fills it full of beer and he goes into the village, and he says, 'Now, you see, this is a piece of paper and what you say here is that you're going to make a little cross there, and here's a beer. And I'll come back next week. If you've done that cross, you'll get another beer.' That's how the ANC rules. Now, they have no clue, no clue. *Na, das Volk hat gesprochen*—'The people have spoken. '

And then they come and complain bitterly. And I say, 'You bloody idiots! You have voted for these people! Why don't you hit them over the head if they don't do what you want them to do?' But, you know, their whole attitude toward democracy is, 'Oh yes—you can say any shit that comes into your head. You can say it loud and clear. But, once you've said it, please shut up and go and do what I tell you to do.' That's democracy here.

M: I'm sure it's a lousy system in many ways. But how can you realistically expect a system that has been so corrupt and so wrong-spirited for hundreds of years to be corrected overnight? You simply can't.

R: Overnight? Well, the oldest nation with a bloody democracy is America. How could someone like a Bush ever get in? Tell me. Explain that to me.

M: Well, first of all, many people, myself included, feel that Bush came in illegally. He didn't even receive a majority of the popular vote.

R: Exactly. Exactly. Now you go to Mr. Mugabe and say, 'Hey, what are you doing?' And he says, 'I'm doing exactly what Bush has done. Go and speak to him.' Thank you . . . no more words to be said.

M: Listen, I myself—and most of the people I know—detest Bush. I think it's a disgrace, and an embarrassment, that he's our President.

R: He's stupid. But the people voted for him—they deserve him.

M: But he got to be President because the election went to the Supreme Court, several of whom had been appointed by his father. And the Supreme Court decided.

R: Now, is the Supreme Court infallible? Somebody probably got a bit of money out of that.

M: Well, you have a system composed of human beings and it's fallible.

R: So what are we arguing about? We get what we deserve. We moan and groan and perform, and lay down our lives for *Volk* and Fatherland and flags and I don't know what, and next week somebody says to me, 'You bloody fools—you shouldn't have done that!' [Laughs.]

M: But sometimes, every once in a while, something good happens, doesn't it?

R: Like what?

M: Well, look at the United States, for example. Just look at its history. Once, blacks were slaves; women couldn't vote. Now, blacks are free, they and women can vote, and . . .

R: And you have laws allowing gay marriages. . . . What next? [Laughs.] Listen, I'm not prejudiced. It's just, are you saying here, 'Listen, all these wonderful things happen.' [Laughs again.]

M: The fact is that there seem to be an awful lot of people in the world—you and I might not be among them—who prefer the same sex to the opposite one.

R: Well, that should be their private joy. Why make a big thing out of it? I mean, who ever asked my grandmother what she did in her bed?

M: But it has a lot to do with how you run the rest of your life. Being married, for example, has to do with having certain rights, with being entitled to certain financial advantages and insurance, and so on.

R: Listen, if you've got a gay relationship, all you've got to do is make a will and put everything in that person's name. You don't have to get married to them! Especially the way marriages are today. How long do they last? The whole thing is a farce, as far as I am concerned. It's their right to do it—with pleasure—but I laugh about it. And you say, 'Look what we've achieved.' [Laughing.]

M: Well, isn't it better to have black people who are not slaves? Isn't it better to have women who have the same rights as men? Isn't that a bit better than it was before?

R: Okay, so let's take it one step further: Wouldn't it be better if animals had the same rights as we have? It's coming one day. They're talking about the great apes getting human rights. I mean why the hell would we say that an animal—a creature with the same feelings we have—is a creature that can be owned? It's the same thing as slavery: You can kill it, you can eat it, you can do what you like with it, you can give it away. Is that right?

M: No, not at all. But I don't by any means agree with you about everything. There are a lot of things I do agree with you about, but quite a few that I don't. But that's all right. What I find interesting is that you're an individual human being with individual experiences and an individual history and individual character traits and individual plans. That's what makes people different, you know? And that's also what's wrong with affirmative action: We take a black person, for a person, and we make that person into a generic black person—in other words, we say that all black people deserve an extra break.

R: And they don't.

M: I agree—they don't. But some of them deserve an extra break, no?

R: But, you know, the world is going around and around and, as long as we've had history, there was always inequality, always the underdog and the upperdog. Just as you could always say, 'That's not right.' And yet, it happened. So how do you want to undo that today?

M: You can't undo it . . . at least not all of it.

R: Exactly. But today we are being bloody ruled by the people who make money. So how do you want to undo that? If they don't like the book you write, they'll make it disappear. And there is nothing you can do about it. If they don't like what you say, they shut you up.

My God, when you see what goes on in South Africa. If the previous government had done a fraction of that, the world would have been up in arms. Now, just because we've got a black president, it's okay. Don't talk to me about politics. You know, what really upsets me about myself is that I came here with the same beautiful ideas—that I was going to change it. And we would sit here, I'm telling you, with my black intellectual friends making a wonderful South Africa. Go and just relax: another year and you can do all these things. Where are they today?

M: It's a bit like the '60s were in the United States. We would make the world fair and just, and clean up the air, etc., etc.

R: Exactly. It's just not happening, so let's forget about it. I have never been as big a racist as I am today! Today, I am a racist. I turn around and I say to Bennett, 'You know, you're a stupid guy, you don't think.' Which is true!

M: On the other hand, I was talking to Josephine this morning [one of the two young black women who work for C.A.R.E. doing menial jobs], and she told me she has a daughter, and that she likes to speak English and wants to learn more. And my sense is that she's a poor girl from a poor black family who is really struggling. . . .

R: She's very bright, and if I could elevate her in any way—I try to elevate her as much as I can here. She could go far. But she is not going to go far—not because of the white people suppressing her, but because of the prejudice among black people against females. End of story.

M: She strikes me as someone with a lot of potential.

R: A lot of potential.

M: And she also strikes me as someone who's had the bad luck of being born in the wrong place at the wrong time, and . . .

R: But she can still make something out of herself. And if I can help her in that way, I will be the first one to do it. But she is not by any means representative of the situation. Josephine is without a doubt the most intelligent black person in this whole operation. And I could easily train her as my secretary—she is wonderful in answering phones; she is wonderful in all sorts of things. But I had to send her upstairs to clean the volunteers' quarters because the bloody stupid American volunteers don't know how to pick up their bloody clothes from the floor! And I said to her, "Josephine, you don't go pick it up, but you say to them, 'Pick it up—or else you'll have a scorpion in it!'" And I hope she does it.

M: I think that race relations are just very difficult for most people, white or black. I myself notice that, if I'm in New York and I'm walking down the street on 10th Avenue, and it's night, and there are two white guys walking behind me, I don't think a thing. If there are two black guys behind me, I'm scared out of my mind. All I do is look backwards. We are so brought up with this racism. I don't treat blacks and whites the same way, and I'm all too well aware of it.

R: There are a lot of things that are misinterpreted. In the example you brought up, for example, in that situation in New York, I think the white people are in the majority, aren't they?

M: In America, yes.

R: Well here in this country it's not the same. Most of the people are black, very few people are white.

M: What are the percentages—do you know?

R: I don't exactly know . . . about five percent are white. So it is absolutely unintelligent of our black president—though he is unintelligent, even if he's quoting Shakespeare whenever he can—to say that it is not fair to say that the black people are the criminals. He's an asshole. If there are eighty percent of black people in this country, then—obviously—something like eighty percent of the crime being committed will be committed by black people, because they are there. And if only five or ten percent of crime is committed by whites, it's also because that's the percentage of whites that are there. It's got nothing to do with racism! It's ridiculous, the whole thing. If you bring this point up in any other country, and you take the percentages of the colored, then you can talk about who is a criminal. And I don't really think that, in your country, it's a black problem—it's a poverty problem.

M: It's, as I said, a class problem.

R: Yes, exactly. But if you want to be the president of a bloody country, you should pick that up, and not make a racial issue out of it, like our idiot is doing.

M: But we have the same kind of people in the States as well. People who say that, as soon as a minority person is arrested or accused of a crime, it's racism.

R: But that is so bloody stupid. And unless people do something about it, we'll have big wars over it.

You know, I think it's time for us to go to bed. When I first came here, every time I went away for a while, I brought the guys here another watch when I returned. And they must have thought I was totally mad! Because, once you live here, you can live totally without a watch—your body is simply telling you when it's time to go to sleep . . . and the baboons are telling you when it's time to get up.

Epilogue:
Death of a Naturalist

I spoke to my friend for the last time on Thursday, July 26, 2012, at precisely 4:00 p.m. Twenty-eight hours later, she was dead, burned to death along with her beloved baboon Bobby and two other baboons in the small apartment she kept above the clinic of the Center. She was probably, as I knew her, listening to Beethoven or watching an old movie with a glass of white wine in her hand when she died.

It's only fitting that Rita should have died of what she so frequently described as "human error"—a not-entirely dissimilar way to that in which her husband and daughter perished some forty years ago. For them, it was a small plane crash; for Rita, it was a fire. Both cases had something, no doubt, to do with "human error."

I had called Rita on that Thursday because, unable to get hold of her for months either by email or phone (not unusual in the South African bush), I had become worried about her, and so I had emailed her colleague Karen Pilling in Johannesburg.

"Hi Michael," Karen immediately wrote back to me, Great timing! After weeks of no phone/Internet service, CARE's line came on yesterday and Rita called me just before I hopped on a plane to London and Zurich. I told her you'd sent a message checking if she was still alive and kicking. She mentioned having written to you about two

months ago in reply to your mail. Now she's doubting whether it
sent? She was touched you were being persistent so please try again!

Regards,
Karen

Which is precisely what I did, just the day, as it turned out, before
Rita would die. "Oh, Michael," she said just before we hang up, "you
needn't worry about an old gal like me. If anything is wrong, you'll
surely hear about it more quickly than if things go right . . . especially
here in South Africa."

And so it would be. Just the next morning, in fact, when the following email, with the subject line "Rita Miljo," arrived from a to-
me-unknown correspondent:

Michael,

My name is Matt Schudel, and I'm a reporter at the *Washington
Post*. We have learned that Rita Miljo, the subject of your story in the
Post magazine on Oct. 19, 2008, has died in a fire in South Africa.

I'll be preparing an obituary.

Do you know if there might be any photos available of her? For
some reason, we do not seem to have any archived photos from your
story.

Thank you for any help you can provide.

Rita was right again: *Human error*. And bad news does indeed
travel fast.

I am a poet in most of my publications, so I don't use words—
especially such tritely overused ones as the word 'love'—easily, or

lightly. I didn't *love* Rita Miljo—she was, after all, as I believe my writings and interviews with her have already indicated, not an easy person to love. No one with her attitudes about her fellow humans—"The worst thing you can do to me," she once told me, "is to make me work with other human beings"—could have been.

But I *did* feel a deep connection, and a profound admiration, for her, as well as abiding sense that here dwelled a unique and genuine human being, a being with a great deal of love in her heart, not necessarily for humans, but, as it was, for baboons, and other animals as well.

Rita and I, I can say with some modesty, hit it off. Perhaps in part because we were so radically different. I have a somewhat sentimental nature, a weakness for my fellow humans, an inherent fear of snakes, crocodiles and large male baboons with their fangs bared. I have never shot, much less owned, a gun, nor can I ever imagine myself aiming one, in less than the most heinous circumstances, at one of my fellow human beings. I've never been in the Hitler Youth.

But what made Rita Miljo both lovable and unique, what drew me to her originally and kept us friends these past five years, albeit over long distances, was the fact that I sensed in her an utterly genuine and utterly honest human being, one incapable of falsity or flattery or the kind of dissembling that gets many of us so far in the more "civilized" world. She reminded me, rather, of some lines from the poet John Berryman's *Dream Song 239*:

> Am I a bad man? Am I a good man?
> —Hard to say, Brother Bones. Maybe you both,
> like most of we.

Rita, to put it simply, was real. She was both, "like most of we." To put it even more personally and simply, I would have trusted her with my life (unless, of course, it came to her choosing between me and a baboon).

When I left C.A.R.E. on that late May day five years ago, Rita walked me out to my car (which the baboons, while I was inside visiting with her, had nearly dismembered), gave me a hug, and said this to me:

"I know this wasn't easy for you, and not at all the kind of life you came from"—a notorious piece of understatement—"and that at times you even felt like leaving. But I admire you for sticking it out, and for being such a good trooper."

I don't think any words of praise have ever meant so much to me.

Then she went on: "I don't think we will ever see each other again. But I do hope we will stay in touch, and I have admired very much the writings of yours I've read. It's funny, isn't it? A Jewish boy from New York and a former member of the Hitler Youth becoming friends in South Africa."

And so, indeed, it was: both funny and beautiful, and a friendship I will remember, with deep affection and gratitude, all the days of my life. Rita was one of the most unusual and least self-involved human beings I have ever known. I can very well imagine, in fact, that she may have died trying, at her own peril, to rescue some of her orphaned baboons, who shared her residence with her, from the very flames that immolated her. It was always clear to me that she valued their misunderstood lives above any human one.

Probably even her own.

She was buried two days after her death on the hill right beside her beloved baboons in a casket shared with the creature on this earth she probably loved most: Bobby, the first battered chacma baboon she ever rescued.

May she rest in peace, as she deserves.

5 August 2012
Hegymagas, Hungary

If you would like to help continue Rita's legacy for baboons you can do so in the following ways:

Visit the C.A.R.E. website: www.primatecare.org.za where you can find out about:

Volunteer opportunities & how to spread the word about C.A.R.E.,
Holding a table at your school or university,
Putting up a poster at your school or university; you can find samples on the website,
Becoming a member of the C.A.R.E. family,
Sponsoring a baboon,
Sponsoring the immunisations of a baboon,
Sponsoring the contraception program at the Center,
Making a donation online.

Spread the word of our cause by joining the C.A.R.E. Facebook page and sharing the posts: www.facebook.com/CARE.baboon.rehabilitation

To contact C.A.R.E.:
Email address: info@primatecare.org.za
Tel: +27 716925055
Post: PO Box 1937, Phalaborwa, 1390, South Africa

Ways to make a donation:
Via the website; www.primatecare.org.za
Via PayPal. Go to paypal.com; under the Transfer tab you will see 'send someone money.' It is a secure site and we have never had any problems. It then brings up a page with a *from* (where you put in your email address) and then a *to* (where you please put in our fundraising email address: donate2carebaboons@gmail.com) and click *continue*. The website itself changes slightly regularly but the concept of sending is usually easy to navigate; it will then take you through how to set up so that you can send money asking for your card details etc.

If you have any trouble please let C.A.R.E. know.

Every little bit helps, everything adds up to make a difference.